POLITICAL ECONOMICS UNDERSTOOD

A Voter Understanding of Lies and Tricks of Politicians

Thomas E. Bird. A.B.; MBA

Order this book online at www.trafford.com
or email orders@trafford.com

Most Trafford titles are also available at major online book retailers.

Printed in the United States of America.

ISBN: 978-1-4669-2302-7 (sc)
ISBN: 978-1-4669-2303-4 (hc)
ISBN: 978-1-4669-2301-0 (e)

Library of Congress Control Number: 2012906066

Trafford rev. 04/05/2012

 www.trafford.com

North America & international
toll-free: 1 888 232 4444 (USA & Canada)
phone: 250 383 6864 ♦ fax: 812 355 4082

CONTENTS

Preface...vii

Chapter 1—Overview and Purpose 1

Chapter 2—Obfuscation 6

Chapter 3—The Political Economy........................20

Chapter 4—Control...35

Chapter 5—The Major Problem 44

Chapter 6—Budgets, Spending and the National Debt........52

Chapter 7—Dealing With Ideology and Political Parties.......68

Chapter 8—Who Are We? 77

Chapter 9—What are "They" really Saying? 86

Chapter 10—The Purpose of Political Parties.....................94

Chapter 11—Some Ideas on Candidates 100

Chapter 12—So Where Are We Now? 108

Chapter 13—What Do We Change?...................115

Chapter 14—The Process of Change 122

Chapter 15—Into Action...................................132

PREFACE

Why write another book about the current economy when book stores are already full of dozens of others expressing qualified opinions on everything supposedly affecting our current economic debacle from religion and morality to the impact of law and regulation or whether the economic theory of Keynes or Laffer is the correct solution.

I wrote it because, like you, I am concerned with the economic condition of the country: not simply the budget deficit; the national debt; unemployment; GDP growth; Medicare; Medicade; Social Security . . . etcetera, etcetera, etcetera, but because of the total lack of understanding of even educated people of what is happening. Also, like you, I am bombarded continuously with opinions of the media talking heads, radio talk shows and both major parties plus the libertarians and Tea Partiers. Conversations with friends, family and business colleagues have convinced me that because we are continuously subjected to the rhetorical bombardment of all these groups, we are confused. This confusion was clearly demonstrated by the November 2010 elections when we voted for individuals running on policies that will most likely make our major problems of GDP growth, unemployment and deficit spending much worse. And that's just the short term period of 1 to 3 years, only God knows what these people will do to long term programs like Medicare and Social Security. The worst part is the Tea party and others told us they were going to cut taxes and social benefit programs to reduce national debt; however, they neglected to tell us about the negative impact on GDP and unemployment. Rather than deal with the "how" of that would occur, they wrapped it in a rhetorical blanket of fear: "we're going bankrupt; but, we'll save you with our austerity programs." and "Let's take our country back". Back from what? I am sure we don't know.

I am convinced that most of this constant flow of rhetoric is deliberate mis-information designed to control our thinking. I further believe we intuitively understand we are being manipulated and this understanding is at the heart of the anger and divisiveness rampant in the United States today and because we do not know how to deal with our frustrations and anger, we simply react unfortunately, often with less than good judgment.

I believe that if we continue to be a nation easily swayed by this constant rhetorical bombardment, just as Germany was in the 1930's, we will simply do the bidding of our economic masters just as the German population did. Remember they are "masters" because they hold the key to the success of their agendas in the form of unlimited funds to finance the cost of convincing us to accept and support their self-serving rhetoric and fallacious logic; and, they are committed to succeed.

Quite simply I am convinced that if each of us understands the facts and their potential impact on us and our country and we are committed to choosing what's best for our country, we will make the right decisions and vote rationally and intelligently. We do not need the interpretation of talking heads and politicians to choose for us. I am fervently opposed to the media that is constantly spinning facts to suit their sponsor's purposes; and, when that isn't enough to sell their sponsors' and owners' programs they simply re-write the facts when they feel it is necessary. I am perfectly capable of making good decisions with clear facts and so are you. There are unbiased places for us to go for clear, honest factual information and they are easy to find.

Regardless of your background or education I want to share with you what I have learned through a long career in business and, in my later years, the same information I share with my college students. I will make it simple and straightforward and give you the tools you need to decipher what is being "sold" as what's good for America.

I want to give special thanks to my wife, Pat and son Brian for encouraging me to attempt to write this book. Without that strong encouragement I probably would have done what so many of us do when faced with something we want to avoid—simply forget it. For those who do read on, please accept what is expressed ahead for what I intend it to be—my attempt to help resolve a bad situation.

The Author

CHAPTER 1

Overview and Purpose

My father and mother were typical hard working "blue collar" people marrying in 1926 and raising a family during the Great Depression. Although limited in schooling they had a deep appreciation for education and instilled it in their three children. My older sister, Betty, completed a college nursing program and became a Registered Nurse; I was the first university graduate in the family with both a BA and MBA followed by my younger brother, John, who completed the same basic education and earned similar degrees. All of us worked our way through college. As a result of my own experience I believe the tools to make sense out of our current problems are within the reach of all of us if we understand where these tools are located and how to use them.

My roots are working class and I know and understand the working family economics; the dedication to improving the lives of our children; and our tremendous patriotism and loyalty to our country. I have also worked as a senior manager in three Fortune 200 companies, as a CEO to two smaller firms and management consultant to over one thousand large and small businesses. I am fully conversant with business and economics and convinced the average working family is fully capable of making sound decisions given the truth. What we are experiencing today is deliberate obfuscation and distortion of that truth by individuals and parties with their own agendas and those agendas are not what is best for the United States.

What I am offering is a methodology to get past the misinformation to the truth supported by facts and history and will demonstrate some simple methods to show you how to separate the policies of left and right, find the solutions that will benefit our country and help us strengthen it. Only by doing this will we be able to pass this country of ours on to future generations as the land of opportunity and freedom for them as it has been for us.

I want to make clear at the outset I embrace no political party; I am concerned with the rhetorical "talking points" the leaders of all the parties consistently pound at us as the "right" course for our country even though these "talking points" are often nothing more than expressions of illogical thinking, prejudiced rhetoric, dishonest representation of the facts and attempts to re-write history to support their positions.

For more than forty years I was member of the Republican Party dutifully voting for most Republican candidates from Eisenhower in 1956 to Bush in 2000. I resigned from the party in 2001 when I saw what Bush was doing and the Party's absurd shift to the right that he was advocating. When I looked at the Democrats response to what was occurring I saw they were no different, except their shift was to the liberal left. Each group in its own way causes as many problems as it fixes and because each party has its own agenda that supersedes the peoples' business, we thus pay extra to conduct the people's business when it is conducted at all. The only reason congress was organized in the first place was to do the peoples' business and now, more often than not, what is done is either counter to the best interests of the people or nothing gets done at all. As a result we ordinary citizens pay a huge price because each Republican, Democratic or Libertarian political agenda has a large price tag for us as a nation. Alas, we must now, in 2012, buy into a long-term government created political-economic program to get out of this mess, or the hole if you prefer, in which we currently find ourselves. The congress and the last administration created most of it and now they offer the same old programs that got us in this mess as the vehicle to get us on the road to recovery and prosperity. If we choose programs and representatives incorrectly the hole will become so deep we will never be able to dig our way out. The price for that failure will be to lose the nation we love and end up with exactly what our founders tried to avoid.

The goal of these parties is political and economic control of our country in order to re-shape it into their respective versions of utopia, ignoring the fact that the world at large has already judged our country as the world's the most admired nation. If we listen carefully to the messages of the parties' leaders, interpreted by reference to unbiased facts, the liberal left version means more social programs like a National Healthcare plan; tough regulation of business; rebuilding America's infrastructure; green energy and tax reform aimed at redistributing wealth back to the middle class with elevation of the lower class poor through education and job training. The goal is more rapid growth and improved jobs for all economic groups; in other words to build a larger, stronger middle class and improve upward class mobility. The probable price is larger government, higher taxes on the rich and deficit spending for the next decade at least.

If we analyze the messages coming from the right wing conservatives they tell us they want much the opposite: low taxes for the wealthy to continue the shift of national wealth to the super rich, assuming it will "trickledown" and restart the economy and not simply increase business's and the super-rich's economic and political control. Additional goals are reduction of government through outsourcing and reduction of government services; outsourcing and reduction of Social Security and Medicare—so called "privatization"; and privatization of education and elimination of controls on business. The probable outcome of such policies will eventually result in a two class economy of rich and poor with few in the middle according to most economists. We may pay lower taxes but give up social programs and have slower growth as a result. Given the recent Supreme Court decisions the political/corporate complex will have all the money it needs to control federal elections not only of the President of the United States and Congress but of State Governors and State Legislatures as well. Elimination of class action lawsuits will reduce the power of the people to fight back and the super rich and corporations will control government programs and laws to support their agenda.

If your goal is the right wing, economic/political two tiered model above you can stop reading now. We are well on our way to achieving it. Given one more election like the 2010 debacle, we will be on a course that promises to be irreversible. I am not suggesting you vote by party nor am I suggesting spending cuts are bad, but I am suggesting we vote only for programs that support our goals and only for candidates that fully support those programs. Understanding what each party and each candidate offers as policy and where he/she stands on specific issues and their impact is the goal of this book. This understanding of intent and content of legislation and political leaders will allow us to make good choices and find the best course for our country. I further suggest that only by learning the simple methods of separating fact from prejudicial rhetoric and misinformation will you be able to fully evaluate the policies of candidates and exactly what they will do regarding the issues at hand; and most importantly, what those actions will do to our country and our economics depending on how they are decided. If informed decision making is your goal then read on!

CHAPTER 2

Obfuscation

to confuse, bewilder, or stupefy.
to make obscure or unclear: to obfuscate a problem
with extraneous information.

Webster's dictionary.

Ignoring the question

Whenever I watch the Sunday morning talk shows I am reminded of the Broadway Toni Award winning musical "Best Little Whorehouse in Texas". In it, one number portrays the governor of Texas being interviewed by the media cleverly not answering questions by dancing around and offering unintelligible responses that are totally off-topic It is appropriately titled "A Little Sidestep" and it was immensely entertaining in the show; however, it is immensely irritating when real politicians are asked important questions about our government, our economic and political problems and their various political positions and beliefs and they do a "little sidestep".

A case in point was the appearance of Congresswoman Michelle Bachmann on "Meet the Press" in early March of 2011. Ms. Bachman was asked several questions by the host, David Gregory, ranging from her intent to take a hard line on the budget before congress by voting against the Federal debt ceiling and possibly shut down the government to her aspirations to be president of the United States. On each occasion she responded with her OWN agenda statement, "Obama stole $105 billion from the people of the United States". Not only did she not address the questions of Mr. Gregory, she offered no factual support for her statement other than "he snuck it through on the 'Obama Care' bill". Although she obviously felt her answers were proper for one in her position, those individuals who do not agree with her would say she was guilty of deliberate obfuscation of Mr. Gregory's attempts to get to the truth of the various matters he raised. Ms Bachmann "sidestepped" his questions by use of the red herring fallacy of casting unsubstantiated aspersions on Mr. Obama. Whether one supports Ms. Bachmann or not it is quite clear she used some well known fallacies and rhetoric to avoid the truth and, in doing so, deprived all Americans of information necessary or at least helpful to understand those areas of concern; and, she replaced valid arguments with invalid arguments based on misinformation.

So how do we deal with situations like this? How do we get to the truth and how do we determine the importance of any given situation? Let's look at how we might react if we did NOT listen carefully and then look again as if we did listen carefully and apply some basic analytical tools.

If we are Bachmann, or Republican, supporters or even committed independents opposing "Obamacare" our reaction might be to believe her; after all she is a Congresswoman. Maybe the president had done something bad, perhaps illegal, and maybe he is even impeachable. If we were Obama, or Democrat, supporters we might react by believing that her statements are slanderous and made only to wantonly discredit the President. In each case our initial reaction is pre-programmed by our rhetorical political beliefs. We reach our position by jumping directly to our conclusion without benefit of really hearing what has been said and understanding what has transpired. Even if we reached the correct conclusion we would not know why, and we need to know why.

So let's pretend we did watch and listen carefully and look at it critically.

First, we need to know exactly what took place. In this case when Ms. Bachmann agreed to appear on "Meet the Press" it was ostensibly to openly and honestly discuss important political issues of the day. However, her behavior on the show when she was questioned clearly demonstrated she obviously had no intention of answering Mr. Gregory's questions, she had her own agenda and it included accusing President Obama of something. We know all that just from observing her behavior. When questions are not answered directly and fallacious statements, so called "talking points", are offered in response we can assume the respondent, Ms. Bachmann in this case, has another purpose in mind. Second, her response would be classified as a "Red Herring" fallacy, or a statement that has no relation to the question but is made to take your attention elsewhere. In this case that the president has done something illegal. Third, the statement that "Obama stole $105 billion from the American people" is at best a weak argument with a premise based on opinion not fact. There is no supporting valid third party reference and as such it is classified as rhetoric, in this case as "prejudiced" rhetoric. In other words, Congressman Bachmann is saying she wants us to accept and agree with what she says, even though it is without factual support. She expects us to agree with her because SHE said it. In HER perfect world perhaps we would do that, but today's real world of politics is far from perfect and certainly statements such as Ms. Bachmann's are not to be accepted without careful consideration of the facts of the matter.

So where are we? We have reviewed Ms. Bachmann's responses, concluded she did not address the questions for reasons that we believe fit her personal agenda and then she attempted to focus our attention on an allegation she made against the president that was unsupported by facts. The next logical step is to investigate the reasons she may have had for her actions. What information is either generally available in the reliable media or verified by competent, unbiased sources that would help us understand her logic. When we check with the Congressional Budget Office we see the funds Ms. Bachmann says are stolen are in fact monies previously approved in the 2010 Health Care reform bill passed by congress after over one year of debate. The $105 billion in question is the amount to be appropriated in 2011 and does not reflect any other budget reductions made in areas covered by the new law. It is clear that there was no sneaking and no theft and this is factually true. In fact the CBO concluded the healthcare law will save $200 billion over the first 10 years after implementation.

Let's return to her statement regarding the $105 billion "theft" by Obama. What does she have to gain from such a statement?

We know from major media coverage including video and direct quotes that she is a committed adversary of the Democratic Party in general and President Obama specifically. We know that congress had president Obama's 2011 proposed budget on the floor and was debating passage and we know that Ms. Bachmann is the self-appointed chairperson of the ultra-conservative Tea party caucus. We also know that she supports major cuts in President Obama's appropriations budget for 2011 and is dedicated to repealing "Obamacare". If we then review specific media, some biased for and some against the President we can consider their inputs using the same factual analysis and thus reach a conclusion regarding what Ms. Bachman said and did not say during her short interview. Using all these inputs we can establish several scenarios that explain her actions:

1. Her Tea party members expect her to vigorously attack President Obama's budget on the grounds it is out of control spending creating a government run Health Care system. This is also unsupported by facts. What is true is the law provides for mandatory coverage through insurance companies with some federal support for hardship. This is verified by reading the law.

2. She is exaggerating the situation in order to bias people and gain support for larger budget cuts and possibly for future career reasons. (i.e. she wants the presidency and announced her intentions a few weeks later.)

3. She truly believes her allegation is true

At this point all facts point to some combination of 1 and 2. Assuming she has a competent staff, and they and she are fully aware of the CBO report she should know her allegations are false.

So now we understand exactly what's going on behind the scenes and what the real issues are. We can now make a preliminary decision regarding Ms, Bachmann's agenda and whether we agree with it. But since the real issue is government spending and whether to reduce it we will need to know exactly what cuts are proposed and their impact before we agree to support her agenda. If any elected Congressman responds to specific questions with a "little sidestep" when questioned on these issues we will need to go through the same steps.

Acknowledging the Question

Obfuscation takes other forms as well. On Sunday March 20, 2011 Admiral Mike Mullen, Chairman of the Joint Chiefs of Staff, was interviewed by David "Gregory on Meet the Press" regarding the US role in the United Nations decision to establish a "No Fly" zone in Libya. As he responded to the primary question of exactly what was the mission he persistently downplayed the US leadership role, emphasizing over and over that it was a coalition whose sole purpose is to stop the killing of innocent non-combatants by Ghadafi' s Air Force. Each time Mr. Gregory attempted to gain a clearer perspective, Admiral Mullen answered directly but always included: it is a UN operation to save lives; it is a coalition including the Arab league; it is limited and not a war with Nation Building as an objective.

The positive thing is he answered questions directly. What makes us uncomfortable is his assignment or agenda, was obviously to convince the host and the American people of the administration's message the talking point: "No Fly" zone, is to save lives; it is a United Nations coalition including the Arab league; it is limited in its objectives and not a war with Nation building", pounds that message home.

People generally agreed with this action, or not, along party lines. The primary reasons given for agreement are: Libya is a threat to our security; Ghadafi is a vicious dictator killing his own people and should be removed and his people want and deserve a democracy. Those who disagree cite our track record of two long wars in the Middle East, with nation building in both cases; the claim that Libya is no threat our security; that this is a civil war in a sovereign nation and not our responsibility.

So this is a good clear interview and we should accept and agree with the Admiral's position, right?

Wrong!

We are so used to politicians' "side stepping" questions and responding with "talking points" that we tend to judge a good interview by the simple criteria of answering questions directly. So what was objectionable about the Admiral's responses? Well, like Michelle Bachmann he also had his own agenda. With two wars in progress in Iraq and Afghanistan the US public was clearly not anxious to take on a third major action, complete with nation building, against still another Arab country. So his unspoken agenda was to convince the American people this was a coalition effort to enforce a United Nations resolution. He was advancing the premise that the UN, in response to abused Libyan people and the Arab League, had ordered a cease fire and the coalition air forces, only temporarily led by the US, would enforce the resolution. His conclusion regarding the expected length of our engagement was also a little fuzzy, he simply intimated it would be successful and only for a short time and we should believe him. Presenting an argument without factual support is expressing an opinion. Granted, he is a highly qualified expert in warfare and as Chairman of the Joint Chiefs the logical person to express an opinion as to probable outcome of such an action, but it is still opinion.

I found myself confused after the interview. He addressed each question but withheld as much as he told us. He assumed we knew what our forces were going do and did not give us details of the mission which we now know amounted to supplying air support for the rebels and denying same to Ghadafi. Clearly his reasons for the interview were to "sell" the idea to the American people that the US was acting responsibly and correctly. On one hand I have compassion for the treatment of Libyans under Ghadafi, especially in the weeks leading up to March 20th; however, on the other hand should we intervene in the internal action, in this case a civil war? In order to better understand the situation I started as we did with Ms. Bachman, by trying to understand the real agenda and reasons for it.

Let's review the facts as supported by the media:

1. Ghadafi was reported by the world media to be a vicious dictator who purportedly ruled with and iron hand.

He had sponsored terrorists as far back as the 1980's and attempted to develop atomic weapons which he abandoned a few years ago. This is well documented in the worldwide media.

2. There was a rebellion in progress with the goal of overthrowing him. This was considered a civil war by most observers. Ghadafi controlled the army and air forces and was using them to kill his own countrymen without regard for their participation in the rebellion.

    a. The United States has a poor track record of intervening in Civil wars and deposing dictators, and rebuilding nations. i.e. Viet Nam and Iraq.

3. The United Nations, at the urging of the Arab League and the US, had issued a resolution to intervene by ordering a cease fire and establishing a "No Fly" zone implemented by member nations including the US to enforce the order.

    a. Implementation had included attacking all targets associated with command and control of military forces and any air defenses that threatened our pilots, including ground targets of tanks and artillery effectively giving the rebel forces air support while denying it to Libyan forces.

4. Various government agencies (Secretary Gates of Defense, NSA and CIA) had independently concluded that Libya was not a threat to the security of the United States.

5. President Obama is on record as late as March 21, 2011 stating the US policy included Ghadafi out of power. He is concerned that his administration may be considered the aggressor internationally and not financially prudent by his domestic opponents. To de-fuse these criticisms he had gained UN support and formed a small coalition of countries to support the United States. This is inferred by a review of recent speeches and articles recorded in the media.

   a. Initial reactions from congress question the constitutionality of ordering US forces to attack without consulting congress. Critics base this on Article 1; Section-8 of the constitution which says only congress can declare war.

   b. Those in favor say this is not declaring war and is provided for in Article 2.

The weight of this analysis says the Admiral obfuscated by not fully divulging all the facts and in fact attempted to present a biased, or prejudiced, argument to support the administration's action to intervene for humanitarian reasons rather than the goal articulated by President Obama of removing Ghadafi from power. In simple language he did not tell all the facts; he deliberately withheld some information while emphasizing other facts. Further, he presented a weak argument for the expected duration of the intervention and did not fully explain the details of the mission.

In this case we look to actions, i.e., providing air support to eliminate Ghadafi' s use of air support for his army and also by assisting the rebels efforts against Ghadafi by striking any military target that may be considered potentially dangerous to our aircraft, which covers most everything. We also look to President Obama's statements clearly articulating that we want Ghadafi out of power. Our actions are more consistent with the goal of ousting Ghadafi than simply humanitarian intervention. Now make you can your decision regarding support for the action based on the facts.

These two examples of obfuscation represent only two methods used by officials. The list is much longer. What is important is you now know how to figure things out when you run into these situations. In today's world we are deluged with opinions from all sources: the internet; politics; talk shows and other media. Presidents speak to us directly and through their aides, press conferences and State of the Union addresses. Congressmen communicate directly and through their aides and associates and bring well rehearsed "talking points" to talk shows, the floor of congress and town hall meetings. We are literally inundated with political manipulation and to make matters worse we are subjected to the talking heads of the left and right and their ever ready interpretations of exactly what this all means and how it supports their various agendas. Most often there is wide disagreement between left and right, little concern for facts, prior experience and what history teaches. Who we are and what we stand for gets lost in the special interests and the wealth to dominate the media. The simple fact of the matter is we frequently don't know who to believe and trust and we need to understand what's happening to knowledgeably exercise our only control, our only safeguard—our vote. The question is how to use it to ensure what is best for the United States.

Remember, organizations have longevity beyond just a few years and with the money available to promote special interests and favorable treatment by the Supreme Court, there are no limits for large institutions other than the size of their bank accounts, especially if current anti-trust laws are not enforced. They can and will dedicate themselves to long term programs. The super rich for example have successfully shifted the wealth to their end over the last 30 years and now control over 80% of the national wealth of the United States. They have accomplished most of this through shifting more of the total tax liability downward to the middle class and below, creating more poverty each year. We have one defense—our vote. If we are to preserve this nation as we know it, we must learn to use it and that means we can no longer allow those in power to manipulate us. To stop this we must find the truth and support for office only those that also share our views—remember they work for us, not the lobbyists and super rich. Dealing with Obfuscation is only step 1. There are other equally effective methods used by politicians to not only avoid answering questions but also shift responsibility and put the questioner on the defensive, such as "Attack and Blame".

During the Republican Presidential Primaries in early 2012 some of the most vicious personal attacks in recent memory were launched by the various candidates. In Iowa Mitt Romney was personally attacked by Newt Gingrich with a series of TV ads and that action drove the caucus away from Romney, who enjoyed almost a 2 to 1 poll advantage only a few days before the voting, to a virtual unknown Rick Santorum. Mr. Romney seemed to have no defense, he seemed flustered when confronted with Mr. Gingrich's charges and thus the direct attack of Mr. Gingrich was successful causing conservative Republicans to shift support to Mr. Gingrich in later primaries. When Romney vigorously attacked Newt Gingrich in South Carolina a few weeks later referencing Gingrich's personal life, failed Speakership and integrity as a businessman he failed to create a similar problem for Mr. Gingrich. Why?

Without trying to determine if all the charges that flew back and for the were true or not, let's focus on why Mr. Romney was severely harmed in Iowa and Mr. Gingrich seemingly grew stronger in South Carolina. It's really pretty simple: Romney lost the "Presidential" look. He seemed weak and unsure of himself and was clearly on the defensive which hurt him in a variety of ways. Already accused of being a weak "flip-flopper" and not "conservative" enough he now looked weak and indecisive plus several defenses he offered were questionable. So the attacks worked to reduce his support for the nomination.

What about Mr. Gingrich? Newt Gingrich is highly skilled at debate and the use of rhetoric and fallacies to win his points; and chief among them this is a technique called "Attack and Blame". Whether it was the Television mediator of a debate or a fellow candidate, Mr. Gingrich vigorously attacked the questioner either ignoring the question or charge all together or denying the specific question or charge and then after placing the questioner on the defensive by admonishing the him or her then, shifting to his own agenda, skillfully gaining control of the interview and scoring the significant points of his program. Voters saw him positively as a result. They saw him as confident, strong, and well-informed; and, even though he differs in several key areas from the right wing of the party, Conservatives saw him as conservative, or at least more conservative than Mr. Romney.

Is he any of those things? I don't know, but his tactics are classic and well-mastered. Why is that important to know? Because I now know he will use key points of the opposing arguments to make his case; and, most importantly, he may or may not believe in his case so I am going to make a great effort to question all of his facts and representations. I will question official numbers he offers in his support and question who his supporters and associates are. I will also review his personal history in similar situations and attempt to learn if he has any conflicts of interest in a given situation. In other words when I see this kind of response to questions and other charges I become very wary.

The important thing is that political campaigning does not present information that tells us what the candidate will do to bring new, innovative solutions to our country's problems; rather it has become a platform to degrade competition through innuendo, lies and other fallacies. It is a battle of defaming people with fallacies and rhetoric the weapons of choice. So what do we do? Once again listen and see if the candidate supports what YOU believe is best and if his approach is "Attack and Blame" or any other rhetorical tactic that demeans and discredits his opponent be especially wary.

CHAPTER 3

The Political Economy

Probably no single subject is discussed more often by more people around the world than the US economy. Everyone has opinions and interpretations of what is currently happening, what's best for the nation now; and, what went on in the past and how that relates to the present and future. Unfortunately, most of these people are biased or simply wrong in many of their conclusions. Many others only report or stress those factors that support *their* conclusions and agendas; and, if the facts do not support their position, they change them, they even re-write history if necessary. Every talk show sends out barrages of misinformation daily to convince us that their party is right about changes that will create jobs for example, and they talk at great length about economic theories that prove their position. Democrats have different ideas than Republicans and even within the two major parties extreme left and right elements have even more unusual and more extreme positions and, of course, the Libertarians and Independents have goals of their own that are just as unsupported as those of the major parties. So what can we do to understand clearly enough to take an informed position on any important issue? Even though everyone can have an agenda and talking points, not all are true and, remember, we are after the truth. Fortunately facts are the elements of truth and as such we can have only one set of facts in any argument. So how do we locate and apply the facts and how do we go about interpreting them?

Let us start by understanding why economics is such an important factor both in politics and in our own lives, then let us spend some time talking about some basic tools to help understand how to find the facts and determine the best course of action for our country and for ourselves.

Why is economics so important? In simple terms it is—MONEY. Or more importantly, it is the creation and use of money. Granted we all need money to live and provide a suitable quality of life for our families and although that is important to all of us, what I am referring to the broader use of money—the creation of national wealth and power. I don't want to get into a detailed discussion of various economic theories but the real power of money is only exerted when it is put to work, actively creating new wealth. With that increased wealth comes the power to improve all facets of living from exploration of the universe to the elimination of disease and poverty. Generation of wealth with its benefits available to all in a politically free environment has been the dream of mankind for thousands of years.

In our economic world today we measure that creation of wealth by Gross Domestic Product or GDP. GDP is a daily subject in the media and congress and both major parties claim they have the answers to all the issues involved and affected by changes in GDP but few ever bother to explain factually how they reach their conclusions. We generally hear only their party talking points and are left only to decide whether or not we agree with their prejudiced rhetoric. In order that we can begin to make our own informed decisions about these important economic questions let's start with a short summary of exactly what is GDP and the relationships between its elements. Once we're clear on these points we'll talk about some of the factors that affect the elements independently, GDP as a whole and the affects on our overall society.

GDP is the total value of all new goods and services produced in our country in a calendar year. It is expressed in current dollars and made up of several components: consumption or consumer spending; government spending; corporate investment and net balance of payments (export-import). Almost 70% is consumption and that's the major drive behind creation of private market jobs; about 20-22% has historically been government spending although it's currently about 25% in the 2011 budget; 15% business investment that actually creates the jobs; and, a negative balance of trade takes us to 100% of GDP.

If the economy is at full employment and we consumers begin to spend less, then producers inventories increase, production slows and jobs are eliminated. By the same token those who provide services have reduced billings and excess service providers and more jobs are eliminated. When this happens, GDP decreases and when it decreases for two consecutive quarters we call it a recession. Then if we consumers begin to spend more, either through incurring debt or government deficit spending then demand for goods and services increases and businesses begin investing in order to produce more goods and services to meet the growing demand. This in turn eventually forces business to create more jobs as they add more capacity. This so called "business cycle" seems simple enough when viewed this way but some other factors are also involved that cause this expansion to eventually lose steam and the economy to slow down again and then repeat itself.

These external factors are not controllable by individual consumers so the federal government has created a number of tools to stabilize the economy.

1. Interest rates play a major role in the availability of consumer loans and investment money from financial institutions. So the Federal Reserve was created in part to implement programs as needed to control interest rates and the availability of money, or "liquidity" for business and consumer loans. For example, increasing interest rates for business investment and or financing consumer purchases will cause a slowing of consumption; and easing of credit will generally stimulate consumption and investment.

2. Taxes can also have a major effect on both consumption and investment. If the government increases taxes on consumers that already spend all they make to stay alive a "fiscal drag" is created by moving that money from consumption to the federal coffers and that slows GDP; if taxes to these consumers are reduced consumption will generally increase as will GDP and eventually employment.

    a. Tax reductions to individuals and businesses that only save these monies from reduced taxes produce no such increase in consumption or GDP and this is only simple re-distribution of income with little or no economic benefit that directly shifts national wealth to the top income earners.

3. If consumption increases, business will eventually react to increases in demand for products and services by hiring new workers.

4. In a similar way competition from low cost foreign producers can slow purchases of US manufactured products as they are replaced by cheap foreign products reducing demand for US manufactured goods thus reducing GDP.

These various actions by government and the Federal Reserve can stimulate or contract demand. Also, this will weaken or strengthen the dollar affecting net exports and the sale of government securities which is influenced by interest rates.

Political Implications

So far it's still a straightforward, but slightly complicated system that responds roughly to supply and demand. If left alone it WOULD eventually respond to supply and demand. The problem is the simple reality that there are a number of other factors to consider that at different times affect all the elements of GDP in positive or negative ways depending on POLITICS. To make matters worse we change our political leadership regularly and since the parties have very different views of the political economy and the role of government we get wide swings of policy. Some times we change the Presidency from Democrat to Republican or vice-versa. Other times we change the majority in congress, in one or both houses. These changes impact priorities, change government goals and objectives, taxation, spending and foreign policy through trade agreements.

We must adjust to accommodate the new directions wisely and for lack of a better word, let's call the total process Political-Economics. It's also important to recognize that contrary to political talking points we have never had a free market economy especially since the early 1900s. Instead we have had a partially regulated or controlled economy; and that control shifts direction from time to time as noted above, even reversing itself, depending on which party is in control. Over the last century when the middle class has increased its share of wealth created we have had long periods of prosperity and when the middle class has seen its share of wealth creation decrease we have seen consumption eventually decrease and entered recessions or even a great depression. Today the economic model is more complicated by the emergence of small, but politically strong, sometimes religiously driven radical special interest groups. These groups have no concept of or obvious concern for the factors that drive job formation and economic growth. Nevertheless they are zealous in demanding their special interests be adapted by the government and forced on all of us, even to the point of damaging the country long term, creating poverty and forcing their ideals on the rest of the population.

Consumption

Economists describe the US economy as "consumption driven". In simple terms increased spending by individuals causes business to expand to provide more goods and services. Conversely, decreases in consumer spending cause businesses to contract and jobs to be eliminated. When there is just enough GDP growth to provide jobs for most people including new workers entering the work force we are said to be at full employment. When this basic balance provides a tax base sufficient to meet the needs of government we have a balanced budget. When net exports do not cause a reduction in employment and all the other factors are as described we are said to be in equilibrium. When tax revenues equal spending in properly planned budgets; the budget is balanced and we do not increase or decrease our nation's debt.

Unfortunately, this balance or equilibrium has rarely been the case in the United States. All sorts of things disrupt the balance from necessary public works to wars, acts of God and welfare needs. Depending on one's political philosophy dealing with these factors may or may not be necessary. We also have had major down turns of economic growth driven by greed and economic control resulting in depressions and recessions. Since the Roosevelt administration in the 1930s the government has funded wars and stimulated the economy with deficit spending by selling treasury certificates: bills. notes and bonds. In peacetime this deficit spending has been to stimulate consumption through job creation driven by investing primarily in large, necessary public works and other programs in part or totally funded by the federal government. Thus the federal government has incurred annual deficits resulting in a national debt currently approaching $16 trillion and the current budget proposed by the administration will result in another trillion dollar plus deficit. To further complicate matters we are attempting to recover from a major recession, fighting two wars and have had a change in congressional majorities and House leadership. All this is causing us to re-consider our priorities and is resulting in some of the most vicious rhetoric in history between the major parties. Regardless of political party those of us who place the United States as first priority need to find a way to first understand which of our elected officials share our convictions and which are committed to any other agenda. To do this effectively we need to understand some of our history and what kind of nation we want to be in the future; and then, after dissecting the rhetoric of our elected officials, determine what our course of action must be. We must then find candidates for congress that share our conclusions and pledge to support them.

The Role of Government

Until the 1900s our economy was described as "laissez faire" and allowed to evolve on its own. The first steps attempted to stop the exploitation of the public by the unscrupulous "Robber Barons" of the 19ᵗʰ and early 20ᵗʰ centuries and to abolish unfair business competition. The establishment of the Federal Reserve by Congress was the first effective effort to stabilize our currency. The Great depression of the late 1920s and 1930s drove the regulation of banks by the Federal Reserve. The stock exchange became regulated by the creation of he Securities and Exchange Commission, the SEC. The most important change in the 1930's was abandonment of "laissez faire" management of the economy by the United States government in favor of the application of the economic principles of John Maynard Keynes, a British economist. Keynes postulated that in depressions the major problem was to stimulate consumption to drive *the economy and create jobs. He clearly pointed out that government spending and recirculation of spending was fundamental, a principle he called the "multiplier". This simple action is nothing more than the government wisely spending where the money will be spent the fastest and change hands rapidly through accelerated consumption transactions. This rapid turnover he called the "accelerator".*

Franklin Roosevelt took over as President in 1933 and employed Keynes' theories through a series of public works programs and is credited with saving the country from a fiscal disaster. He financed our World War 2 costs the same way and presidents that followed him did much the same until the second term of President Clinton in the late 1990s. Focusing on a program of a balanced budget and financed by increased taxes, especially on the high income earners and the technical boom of silicon valley, Clinton actually retired debt and left office in 2001 with a national debt of about $5.5 trillion, a booming economy and a forecast supported by the Congressional Budget Office analysis of total debt elimination by 2010; however, when that date arrived it proved to be a bad forecast as it was implemented; the debt was at $14 trillion and climbing!

What Happened?

The net balance of political philosophy from Presidents Roosevelt through Carter was to work to improve economic conditions and class mobility and thus improve the quality of life of the average American by development of a strong middle class. It always included government deficit spending. Granted we fought WW 2, Korea and Viet Nam and the cold War with Russia and during that period our economy was always driven by military spending; however, we also financed the Interstate Highway system, and put together the greatest, most effective and beneficial government program since WW 2: the NASA moon project. The technical fallout and general wealth increase from that program created the tech world as we now know it with everything from computers to medicine to business management strongly benefiting. It drove the dot com explosion of the 90s and is still is a source of new technology.

The major thing that occurred in the early 2000s was the change in political leadership. After the explosive boom of the 90s, the reduction of national debt and the balanced budget work of the democratic Clinton administration the American voters turned to the opposition party and elected the republican George W Bush, the son of Clinton's predecessor. It was obvious from early on Bush had a different philosophy when it came to the role of government and a much different view of taxation and how it affected the US economy. He pushed through major tax reductions heavily favoring high income earners and within 18 months engaged the country in two wars in Iraq and Afghanistan. He accelerated the de-regulation of Wall Street banks and brokers which eventually resulted in failure of those systems and required him to initiate a massive and unbudgeted bailout of more than $800 billion just before leaving office. When this proved inadequate, it was increased by president Obama in early 2009 by an equal amount to save the major industries of finance and automobile production and to stimulate the economy to save millions of jobs.

After the September 11 El Qaeda attack Bush authorized arbitrary surveillance of, and actions against, suspected terrorists and others violating laws that were passed 30 years earlier during the Carter administration regarding wire tapping. In order to justify his "war on terrorism" he forced through a new interpretation of the Constitution, suspending the right of Habeas Corpus, and amending the Bill of Rights of the United States Constitution, "The Patriot Act". This "amendment" of the Bill of Rights and the Constitution was by act of congress which is not in compliance the methodology spelled out in the Constitution to change the constitution; and thus is in violation of the constitution or unconstitutional. The net result of his two term presidency was to decrease individual freedom guaranteed by the constitution and particularly the bill of rights; increase the national debt from the $5.5 trillion that Clinton left and turn the forecasted elimination of all national debt to a total debt approaching $14 trillion. When he left office unemployment was over 8% and heading to 10.3% before the new administration could reverse the surge. The Bureau of Labor Statistics reports these statistics although analysts think the real rate of unemployment was under-reported and was probably twice that high in reality.

So what did happen or more appropriately what is continuing to happen. If we examine the policies of the administrations and congresses from Roosevelt through Clinton there are some common threads:

1. Even if it has been the nature of the major parties to have widely varying political views the common thread was the common agenda to put the United States first and the political agendas after. Certainly all had their agendas, their pork barrel projects and at times hatred for the opposition but they hung in and put country before party. Today the divisiveness and vitriolic rhetoric of the political parties supersedes all concerns for what is best for the country and what the voters want. These individuals pursue their personal agendas and ideologies. Collaboration seems impossible and even finding common ground for compromise is becoming less possible.

2. Communication and dissemination of information was primarily by responsible media who saw their role as reporters of the news. There were always those TV news anchormen who commented and interpreted the meaning of the news but it was not common to take political positions and "spin" the news. They put country first. Today everyone in media seems to have their agenda and all interpret events to support those agendas.

3. The arrival of the internet, cable "news" reporting like Fox and MSNBC, the birth of internet blogs, Facebook and others gave amateurs and professionals an avenue to reach mass audiences at low cost with any and all

messages, regardless of truth or training. They present their own vested interests and agendas.

Given theses changes and the growing effectiveness of these biased individuals the stage was set to control large groups of poorly informed people by playing on their individual emotions and biases. When the Supreme Court ruled in favor of large corporate political donations in the Citizens United case it gave "Big Money" corporations the chance to financially control federal, state and local elections and squeeze out the candidates who did not play the game the way they were directed. The net result is a deluge of "news" that is in most cases severely biased. The average voter like you and I is left to our gut feel and basic political loyalties to make our choices. I believe all of this to be a valid summary of what has transpired over the last 11 years and it is true to the best of my knowledge. It is the only explanation I can justify to myself to explain how we voted for people in the last election that clearly told us what they would do: reduce GDP, increase unemployment and increase the national debt by 2020 to an amount equal to or greater than the then GDP.

If we return to the first part of this chapter and the discussions of GDP, jobs and stimulating the economy and accept that information as true, we would not vote for candidates that told us they were going to reduce consumption for example. We would not vote for those that promised tax cuts that we had to borrow to give and which did not stimulate the economy to produce jobs, and we certainly would not have voted for candidates who want to take basic assistance programs away from people who have no alternate source of income to feed their families. But the programs and budget cuts that are on the floor of congress today say exactly those things. Republican Congressman Ryan from Wisconsin, Chairman of the House Finance Committee, introduced the 2012 Republican budget proposal to congress and the Republican controlled House passed it; the Democrat controlled Senate did not. The Congressional Budget Office published their analysis that if it is implemented the Draconian cuts to public programs will severely depress economic growth, reduce employment, severely reduce services and increase the national debt by several trillion dollars. Congressman Ryan calls it his "Road to Prosperity" plan restoring financial stability and even though the CBO said differently he repeated his position in the 2013 Republican budget proposal, which also passed the Republican controlled House. We need to examine these proposals carefully and determine whether we agree that they are good for the country and good for each of us and then let our congressional representatives know exactly how we feel.

We expect our elected representatives to debate and argue policy and spending issues. We also expect them to accept laws previously decided and support previously implemented program decisions like family planning. Arbitrarily using archaic senate rules to control of one house of congress to force the will of the minority on the majority because of ideological and religious differences is contrary to the principle of majority rules expressed in the constitution. If the republicans want to change the Comprehensive Heath Care Bill, "Obama Care" passed last year for example; there is an acceptable pathway to change. The same applies to abortion and funding women's healthcare programs.

Threatening to shut down the government by refusing to pass debt limit increases in an attempt to coerce the administration to accept closing and discontinuing Human Services, as affected by the Republican minority "Tea Party", is reprehensible.

It is not the author's purpose to discredit any political party but it is his responsibility to expose thinking that is contrary to the best interests of the United States. I also hope to pass on to you the reader a simple method of separating facts from personal agendas and to help you decide issues for yourselves. I believe if you will stay with me to the end of the book, no politician will ever be able to fool you again, at least not twice as the famous (or infamous) Bushism says . . . "Fool me once . . . ."

CHAPTER 4

Control

From the time of Rome, politics has always had the interlopers who would profit first from their prominent or political positions and only serve their country when it suited their agendas; however, it is worse now than ever and represents the greatest threat to our country since World War 2. We no longer have senators conspiring to assassinate one who is "ambitious" on the floor of the Senate as in the case of Julius Caesar, in order to gain control of government and push their personal political agendas; but we do have senators and congressmen bonding together around minority special interests. Group murder has changed form and now amounts to organized character assassination through attack and blame and highly prejudiced and non factual rhetoric. A good example of this is the ranting of right wing conservatives, "birthers", who attack Obama as being ineligible under the constitution to be president because he is not a US born citizen, claiming he is from Kenya. They further extend this charge to include the even more illogical charges, equally unsupported by facts, that his birth records in Hawaii are false and it was a conspiracy by Muslims to take control of the United States. One of the major promoters of this fallacy was the real estate mogul, Donald Trump.

The facts are indisputable: Obama is automatically a US citizen and eligible to be president because his mother is an American citizen and he was born in Hawaii, end of discussion. But if one argues further his birth records, school records and passport records support his claim of citizenship. So the entire argument of Trump and the "birthers" is based on the false premise that Obama is not a citizen which is untrue. What is truly sad is that more than 25% of people identified as conservatives in recent polls believe the "birther" charges. These facts, plus the illogical premise that people "Planted" Obama 50 years ago and foresaw he would be attractive, articulate, intelligent and able to complete his education on scholarships to three major universities and make the Harvard Law Review as one of the brightest in his class, defy reason. So why do the right wing conservatives and the interloper, Trump, promulgate the myth? Control!

We have to remember that to achieve anything in politics control of the thinking of the "deciders" is fundamental. This is why the "Attack and Blame" fallacy is used so effectively. It allows the politician to discredit his opponent and condition his audiences to support his agenda whether it is good for them or not. Why would Donald Trump make such absurd charges? He has attorneys that will immediately tell him Obama is qualified to be president because his mother is a citizen. No one challenged Senator McCain when he ran for the presidency and he was born in Panama. All this is nonsense about whether Obama was born in Hawaii, or not because it is meaningless. No, Trump did this for his personal agenda of gaining support of the believers of the "birther" myth so he could gain the republican presidential nomination. He later withdrew.

We deal with these fallacies just as we do with obfuscation. We examine the statements for the supporting facts. If they are missing, incomplete or prove false we go one step further and look for the applicable truth, in this case Obama is a citizen by virtue of his mother's citizenship and supporting legal documentation of his birth location, Hawaii. Then we look at alternative scenarios to explain why Trump, in this case, takes his obviously erroneous position. We examine available facts from reliable sources, in this case polls, and we find a plausible explanation based on facts, not personal agenda. In this case, Trump is "ambitious". We can now make a rational decision to support or not support Trump based on other considerations like his qualifications of which there are none.

Control over the citizenry by those who would rule is nothing new. Throughout history people have craved power over the masses. From Rome where the aspiring Caesars connived against and even murdered family members for the power to rule through the medieval Holy Roman Empire where control was effected by Christian dogma promising or denying eternal life then later by "Divine Right of Kings" also supported by Catholic popes, control of men's minds and bodies was the practiced goal. As the western world evolved away from this Divine Right concept, control was effected politically, either through the concept of all sharing as needed in the fruits of the labor of all and implemented by a doctrine fear and punishment as in Communist, Fascist and Nazi societies. In more democratized societies citizens shared in control through the vote and politicians connived to control that vote.

It is important to note that through the reformation and subsequent exploration age when the new world was opened the catholic church maintained indirect control of the ruling class and the general population through the same dogma of promising or denying eternal life and when this control failed to hold the masses in check and prevent formation of protestant sects they declared them heretics and killed them. This resulted in what came to be known as lack of religious freedom and was one of the major driving forces for colonization of the Americas, particularly North America.

It would be wonderful to say that those people who came to the colonies to gain religious freedom also believed others should also be free to choose their religion—or not. Unfortunately the control concept of religious groups is still alive and well as we see in the never ending demand of the religious right that a woman's right to choose, family planning and even sex education of our children must stop. Today intolerance for differences in religious convictions has been expanded to condemn Islam because some of the terrorists who harmed the US were Muslim extremists and obviously Islam was to blame. This concept of control, forcing beliefs on others and condemning sects for the actions of a few, is completely analogous to the persecution of Jews by Hitler, the Spanish Inquisition and the Crusades of the Middle Ages. Whether we continue these practices in our country is a choice we can make. My only suggestion is that we look at our options carefully and wisely and make our decisions rationally.

Rational Decision Making

Why include discussions of rational decision making at this point? It's really straightforward; the number of arguments being delivered in the political economic world are based on all sorts of premises based on all kinds of supporting factual references. Our guiding principles are set out in the United States Constitution which is the contract we, as citizens, have with the federal government. In it we give up certain individual rights for certain group benefits. Disputes of the role of government, individual rights and states rights are governed by the constitution. Our system of law is controlled by it and it is our reference document. When any of our relations with rights and government are involved we have a common authority.

This is very often not the case in disputes of morality, religion, economics, politics and even history. To make matters worse we frequently develop arguments based on opinions of these areas and their meaning to us as a society, not arguments supported by hard facts. Sometimes we attempt to support our positions by reference to materials not generally accepted as guidelines. For example if a Christian and a Muslim are debating religion, reference to the different sacred books is difficult because of no common authority. So it is with political parties and economic theories like those Michael Steele, former Republican National committee Chairman, offered on the April 15, 2011 Bill Maher television program when he claimed "cuts in spending create jobs". Neither history nor recognized economic theory supports that statement. So it is necessary to find common ground for resolution of differences. Exchanging talking points from political agendas does not work.

Rational decision making suggests an organized process: we listen to the argument, determine the premise, consider the suggested conclusion and test it with alternatives. If we are inconclusive in our decision we look for additional facts, 3rd party experiences and arguments of similar cases and decisions and finally history. In the final analysis we may be forced to make the decision by inference. The key points are to be organized and consistent.

Granted, we cannot approach every conversation, TV speech or talking head comment in this thorough complete way; but use of this approach will become automatic if we practice it. As we discussed in earlier chapters, the tip-off is always how the individual is answering questions, making summary statements, and presenting information. Do you clearly understand what the individual is saying? Is he/she direct and honest? Does he/she state their position clearly? The vaguer the statement the less believable it is. Are they obfuscating? Are answers contrary to known information? If you answer yes to any of these questions bore in and do a complete analysis.

For example, both Presidents Bush and Obama were asked at different times during their terms in office about fuel prices and why they were rising. Both answered it was a "supply and demand" problem. Statistics and records of fuel consumption showed clearly in both cases that GDP was flat to down and Americans were driving less and current automobiles delivered substantially higher gas mileage than those that were being retired resulting in slightly decreased consumption of gasoline per mile driven in the United

States. Increased consumption in China and India as suggested by Bush had not totally replaced that demand. The statements were false! Why did they make them? It's hard to say why but from inference we might conclude it was for political control reasons. Both presidents were engaged in other more serious fights at the time and neither seemed to relish the truth that speculation in anticipation of higher oil prices was the major reason and they did not want to risk irritating the rich and powerful; however those working in the Mercantile Exchange were very quick to offer speculation as the reason, going so far as to say it was controllable by executive order. That's a somewhat questionable approach as commodity trading is international and traders and hedge funds had been using the International Commerce Exchange in London England for several years to avoid regulation. In any event neither president issued an order nor did they mention it was possible to alleviate the problem so easily; moreover, elimination by Bush of the long standing regulation that speculators must take delivery if there were no buyers for their futures eliminated most of the problems for the speculator.

Is this dishonesty? On the face it most certainly is. Should we challenge it?—Most certainly!

It was done for reasons of control. Speculation by Wall Street was once again causing problems for the average American family and neither president wanted to face the issue directly and risk the blame for allowing it to continue.

Higher fuel prices are highly inflationary, destroy asset value, reduce purchasing power of money and is really a kind of highly discriminatory "tax" on the middle and lower income families reducing disposable income necessary for other purchases. It also has a very negative impact on GDP as imported fuel is substituted for other purchases of domestically produced products and affects the price of virtually everything we consume. Was there really anything more important for Obama than creation of jobs and recovery from the recession? What could he possibly gain by failing to tell the truth? So he accepted the affects on GDP and inflation and put the blame on foreign growth, in China for example, where we already had generated irritability of the US voter because of currency, job losses and trade issues.

Who knows the specific reasons that caused these presidents to lie to us. By inference we might suspect they were giving into pressure from the oil industry and Wall Street and they concluded it was better to work privately to deal with the problem. In simple terms, they needed the support of these powerful companies to fight other battles, which again is a control issue. One thing is certain; those of us who knew how to research the problem were not fooled. The problem is we could do nothing about it but expose the situation to our own circle of people and protest through letters to congressmen, senators and press. Even worse, this is not an isolated example of dishonesty in government. Most of us have become so used to lies coming out of government we no longer question them and are unwilling to fight for truth. Remember that Constitution we talked about earlier? It is a contract between us the citizens and the government; and we assume there will be full and complete disclosure and the disclosure will be honest. The Constitution goes so far as to say we can impeach these elected appointed officials for high crimes and misdemeanors; and, lying to the citizenry is included in that definition. Yet we do nothing. We allow our representatives, local, state and congressional and even the president to say anything they choose; to adopt any programs they want and govern independently without challenge. I do not believe this is because we are weak. I believe it is because we have accepted these various control tactics and the reason we accept them is because we do not understand how to challenge these control devices used by politicians. The best way to do that is by using the simple analytical process we have been discussing followed by direct challenge. If this doesn't work let's find new candidates and elect them. But to do that we first have some basic things to change.

CHAPTER 5

The Major Problem

When I hear politicians support positions that are illogical and obviously those of special interests groups I am immediately reminded of all that's wrong with our political system. When a US senator or congressman obviously pays his debt for campaign contributions and support by endorsing the views or political positions of these special interest groups, it is demeaning to our entire system and is a clear demonstration of the root of the dishonesty and corruption in Washington. What makes it worse is that everyone knows it and no one does anything about it because those in a position to make the necessary changes, and the individuals, companies and organizations that sponsor them, are the ones profiting by the current situation and they like things as they are. Oh, there have been ineffective efforts like the token campaign reform legislation that John McCain sponsored a few years ago and President Obama campaigned on cleaning up Washington but nothing has been done that has had any affect on the control money has on our lawmakers. Even our president has settled into the system he vowed to "clean up". The recent "Citizens United" decision by the Supreme Court has made an already bad situation much, much worse. In simple terms most of our elected officials are placing personal and special interest groups agendas ahead of the people's business and the three powers, or branches, of government are cooperating to make things worse for the people of the United States. Some call that Washington doing business as usual but I call it corruption and it is the root cause of our present problems including the recession, rising debt, unemployment and loss of personal freedom. It seems the "Tea Party" with there maniacal focus on cutting spending is chasing the tail of the demon rather than confronting him head-on; although since they are also receiving heavy financial support from the multi-billionaire Koch brothers this is not surprising. Regardless of how one frames it, this must stop if we the people are to regain control of our country.

Campaign Money and How to Raise it.

It is public knowledge that congressmen spend about as much, or even more, time raising money for their election war chests as they do working on the people's business. Remember it is the people's business that is the sole reason for their jobs. While campaign funding has always been a problem for elected officials it has grown in recent years to a point that is totally out of proportion to the personal economic value of the job. Candidates, funded by mainly special interest groups, spend millions to be elected to jobs that pay only about $170,000 per year or so. Even though that is a substantial sum it doesn't justify the money spent, and certainly not the time spent, raising the money unless there are other major benefits. Michelle Bachman, one of the most successful congressional fund raisers, has publicly complained she doesn't have the time to read and understand bills like "Obama Care" because they are too large, complex and hard to understand. This was apparently so difficult in the case of Obama Care she said "Obama snuck by and stole $105 billion in his 1000 page bill". She had several months to review the bill and yet she made no comment. Maybe she was busy elsewhere, besides it was written in the House of Representatives by congressmen and their staffs, not Obama. It seems her priorities are totally backward, time for fund raising greater than time for conduction of the people's business, and she doesn't understand who writes the bills in congress.

We need a better method of funding campaigns for federal offices. That method should make raising "war chests" from corporations and wealthy individuals and spending personal funds on elections illegal. We have literally left the foxes, in this case the Congress, Supreme Court and the Administration, in charge of the henhouse. It is time to change that. They should have no say on how they are elected and appointed other than the message they personally deliver. How the campaigns are financed is the people's affair and the people should write the rules. Interpreting free speech to include that of money, as the Supreme Court has done, is ludicrous!

The major question is how to accomplish changing the rules for financing political campaigning without discriminating against potential candidates. One method that has been mentioned frequently is public financing by the taxpayers. Using this method would require careful thinking to avoid problems of potential abuse, profiteering and discrimination; but, with careful analysis and implementation, it would eliminate the stranglehold the special interests groups have on our political system and provide a method for grass roots candidates to make themselves viable in national and local elections. It can also have a beneficial effect on bringing new better qualified candidates into the political arena from established political parties and by freeing them from the both the need to raise money and radical ideologies. Today independent candidates have virtually no chance of becoming known unless they can gain the support of wealthy backers or have those kinds of resources themselves; and, major party candidates are selected by party leaders; so, unless a candidate is supported by major party leaders he has a difficult time making himself known as well. Public financing, with appropriate rules, can give the independent a chance to make the public aware of his abilities and ideas and loosen the stranglehold major parties have on candidate selection. The candidates that can most effectively convince their constituents will win. I am not advocating abolition of political parties, just the control of party bosses on who is best suited to represent those parties' positions to the voters.

When I hear elected officials as important as congressmen and senators support ideas and make statements that reflect on their lack of understanding of economics, political science, international trade and politics I am more and more certain we need to seriously consider revising the qualifications for these high offices, at least qualifying them for public financing. Times have changed dramatically since the constitution was written and the world grows constantly more complex. I would suggest we institute an education or at least and examination requirement to assure candidates possess at least a working knowledge of these key areas. I recognize this would discriminate against those who do not have the educational requirements or the knowledge but don't we already discriminate against those not licensed and admitted to the bar in law and those who do not have a medical degree and pass state licensing requirements in the practice of medicine? I believe our critical senior elected positions in government are at least as important to the people.

Writing the rules for this program is critical and I leave that to the experts with the basic guidelines of taking influential money out of campaign financing with a public financing plan that does not discriminate more that requiring a level of competence necessary to work effectively in that environment and to eliminate potential abuse and profiteering. But there is one other area of concern that we must deal with just as aggressively that is at least as dangerous as campaign financing, and that danger is lobbying.

Lobbying—What Do We Do With It?

Lobbying in the United States is an interesting phenomenon. On one hand the people who make the laws need to know about the effect of proposed legislation and needs of the people and do not have time to investigate each situation in depth. (There's that time problem again). On the other hand organizations, individuals and companies need to make their needs and desires for various programs known. Lobbyists fill that communications gap by working to bring information and needs to the lawmakers and do so for a fee paid by their clients and since each lobbyists represents many clients it saves our representatives time. Without lobbyists each firm and individual would have to represent themselves taking up more of the precious time legislators have available for the peoples' business. So far so good—right?

Wrong! There's that "money is the root" problem again. Over the years the number of lobbyists has mushroomed. Some reports claim the number of registered lobbyists increased six fold under the Bush 2 administration. With all that increase came higher and higher fees and costs with lobbyists competing for time with the "Peoples' Representatives" and of course more money flowed through the system with little or no real control of what was spent and where it went. Ostensibly it went for campaign contributions and other "necessary expenses" that sometimes included junkets for influential congressmen to the golf courses of Scotland for several days to several weeks. Everyone got rich at the taxpayers cost because these lobbying firms exerted enormous influence on the creation of our laws. Was it corruption or not?

The famous, or perhaps we should say infamous, convicted lobbyist Jack Abramoff told the Sunday news program, 60 Minutes, in early November 2011 that he "controlled" over 100 Congressman. Through gifts, contributions and other "perqs" he had the ability to effect legislation important to his client companies. This, from one lobbyist and there are thousands! How bad is the problem? It's bad when a new congressman with limited net worth can become a multi-millionaire in a few short years on a salary of $170,000 per year. In any event between campaign contributions and "necessary expenses" which could include anything from the afore-mentioned junket to stock market tips, lobbying has grown many times over and has an immense impact on what peoples' business is done and most importantly its content. In some cases the lobbyists even wrote the legislative bill for the "overworked" legislator. I suspect those bills favored the lobbyist's client more than the people.

So what do we do? I find the personal gain that politicians derive from lobbyist's activities reprehensible and it must be stopped. I find it unacceptable that a next to penniless young man with limited resources can be elected to congress and 25 years later have a net worth of $35 million on a principle average annual salary of under $170,000. There is just something fundamentally wrong with that. The approach to eliminate corruption and influence peddling so far has been only the minor attempts of preventing money from directly influencing legislators through limited oversight. With public financing of federal campaigns that will improve; however, we also need to put stronger rules in place for the legislators that deal with lobbyists. "Tut-tuts" and wrist slapping are not enough. We need rules that make it a felony for both participants in any scheme where the legislator personally benefits from the contact with the lobbyist and no "necessary expense items". If the legislator travels he travels at government expense on official business with all the limitations on expenses normal for that class of travel. No entertaining, each pays for and accounts for all costs and no gifts for the legislator, his family, his foundation, his library his friends, associates or any other person or place where he could receive even the slightest benefit. No money or equivalent changes hands at any time. And everything must be transparent: all meetings must be in the congressman's office with minutes signed by both parties under penalty of perjury.

Sound too strict? I don't think so. If exceptions need to be made they can be made with full disclosure to appropriate oversight committees and the basic purpose of lobbying will be met.

Remember we aren't taking these measures arbitrarily, congress has demonstrated dishonesty, favoritism and outright payoffs. We need a tightly controlled system to regain operational control our our country.

These two issues are well understood by all members of congress, the administration and the Supreme Court yet no action is taken. The reason for that is simple: very powerful people and organizations both inside and outside government don't want things to change. They are doing incredibly well in every way and they want the wealth to keep flowing their way to increase and intensify their control over us and the wealth and power of the United States. Along with this financial control will come any legislation and law interpretation necessary to strengthen their program. The only defense we, the average citizens, have is to make these fundamental changes as step one—to get the money out of politics. We will probably have to change most or perhaps all of congress to accomplish these tasks but failure to do so will eliminate the United States of America as we know it and eventually bankrupt our treasury and destroy our quality of life.

CHAPTER 6

Budgets, Spending and the National Debt

News media, talk shows and the internet are full of discussions, opinions and predictions about these very important economic factors and a short discussion on the relevance and importance of the current major economic proposals and how they affect them is certainly germane to our analysis and discussions.

Budgets

Let's start with budgets. The fiscal year for the United States government begins on October 1st of each year and ends on September 30th of the following year, So the first year budget of the present administration's first year in office, 2009, actually began over three months before the Democrats took control of government on October 1, 2008. Each year the administration prepares a budget for the following year that includes estimates for future years and submits it to congress for approval and appropriation authority. It includes forecasts of GDP and tax revenues that will occur as a result of the independent management of the economy by the people and the impact of a finite level of spending to implement the strategy of the president. The administration then sends it to Congress which controls the appropriation of the necessary funds as directed by the constitution. The president manages the administration, through the departments, bureaus and agencies, and spends or disperses the money that is approved by congress. The administration's budget is physically prepared by the (OMB) Manager of the Budget and distributed to all congressmen, staff, agencies and offices, including the Congressional Budget Office, (CBO). The CBO is a non-partisan government office charged with independent, non-political interpretation of the financial impact of all proposed legislation on the country. This includes estimates on economic growth, employment and budget surplus/deficit impact through the forecasted period. The CBO publishes its report regarding anticipated results on the economy as an official report to congress and all interested parties. In some cases they will assess the impact as far as 40 years or more in the future if the budget proposal affects the deficit, employment, social security, Medicare and Medicaid that far out. They immediately analyze the proposed legislation and publish a report on the consequences as seen impartially.

Before voting on approval the House of Representatives sends the proposed budget to the house budget committee where it is analyzed and then reported back to the house leadership. That leadership, the Speaker, who is elected by the majority party (currently the Republican Party) and majority and minority party leaders can make any changes suggested by the committee and put it on the floor for debate and vote. If the speaker is not in agreement he may also send it back to the committee, whose chairman is also Republican, for changes and may never allow it to return to the floor for debate.

It is a simple enough system when no serious differences exist but becomes much more complex when the opposing party to the president is in the majority and controls the House of Representatives. It becomes even more complicated when that party submits their own budgetary version of how they think things should be and it differs so significantly from that of the administration that it represents a different strategy, which is the case in 2011. Republican congressman and chairman of the House Budget committee Ryan of Wisconsin has proposed a budget very different than that submitted by the president. He has taken a very harsh position versus programs that support low income and middle class people and also opposes entitlements aiding the aged: including Medicare, and Medicaid which supports the poor, virtually eliminating both within ten years according to the CBO. He has attacked entitlements including Medicare while cutting virtually all expenditures except Defense which he increased. With all this cutting of expenditures he proposes major tax rate reductions of corporate and personal taxes to a maximum of twenty five per cent, which according to the CBO, does not balance the budget until 2050, 39 years from now. The CBO further states the Ryan budget will increase the national debt through 2023 to more than $23 trillion from the current $15 trillion plus. On the other hand the president's budget maintains the entitlements, support for the poor and disenfranchised, grows GDP faster and reduces the debt by $4 trillion by 2023. The Republican House rejected the administration budget and passed the Ryan Republican budget;

however the Ryan Republican budget did not pass the Senate and would not be signed by President Obama if it did; so it appears we are at an impasse and without a 2012 approved budget. The 2013 budget appears headed the same way.

Spending and the National Debt

Spending is authorized by congress and implemented through the administration's Treasury Department. Under the law the Treasury may only expend what congress authorizes up to the approved National Debt ceiling. In the past 10 tears since Bush 2 took office that debt ceiling has been raised nine times. It was increased again in the late summer of 2011 after the Republican, Tea Party controlled, party threatened to shut government down unless the President agreed with cuts to programs affecting the poor, women and elderly. If the major political parties were unable to agree to raise the debt ceiling the Treasury would have been prohibited by law from spending above the debt limit and theoretically payments of US obligations would stop. In reality, some revenues would continue to come into the Treasury and provide some funds for dispersal so selected payments would continue, which debts and entitlements that would be paid would be up to the discretion of the administration based on its priorities but regardless of priorities the result would be bad for the country and us citizens.

It is important to understand these relationships.

Historically, the basic strategy of the president was the driving force behind a final budget passed by congress with arguments and debates generally limited to some of the major issues necessary to implement that strategy. Even under Bush 2, who demanded major, arbitrary tax cuts for the wealthy, started two wars and deregulated the banks and Wall Street, the debates and arguments focused on specific issues, not basic strategies. Since the Obama was elected and especially since the 2010 congressional elections, that has all changed. What we now see is a basic ideological argument between the moderate Democratic Administration and the conservative, Republican religious right wing and Tea Party advocates driving a radical plan for restructuring our country. These two very specific strategies for the United States are so fundamentally different that experts agree they will produce very different long term outcomes financially and socially. It is the differences and the expected effect each would have on our way of life that congress and the administration are debating and it is these debates we must follow and support as we decide what is best for our country, ourselves and our children. We need to examine things carefully and let our elected servants know what we, the people, want.

Understanding the financial expression of these ideological differences is important but understanding how political manipulation of these financial elements affects the outcome of these debates is even more important. Theoretically debate and rational compromise by the parties is good for the country and if all of the decisions made by congress were made that way I would not have been so motivated to write this book. But let's be honest, there are devious tricks and procedures based on outdated rules that aid unscrupulous congressmen and congressional leaders in preventing the will of the people from being enacted. For example, during the congress elected in 2008 the democrats enjoyed a substantial numerical advantage in the Senate and the House because the people had overwhelmingly approved of their campaign promises and elected them; nevertheless they were stopped more than 300 times from even bringing that legislation to a vote because the minority Republican Party disagreed and invoked an ancient and often amended Senate rule called the Filibuster which prevented action by the majority.

The Filibuster was instituted in the 19th century as a Senate rule that allowed a senator to delay votes on issues he opposed so he would have time to gain the necessary support from colleagues and gather votes of opposition; it was not to get around the constitution which calls for majority rule except in the specific instances of impeachment, treaties or constitutional amendment.

This original senate filibuster rule required the senator to stand on his feet and speak to hold the floor; and as long as he could stand and speak he could prevent the other party from bringing the issue to a vote. Anyone who saw the 1939 movie "Mr. Smith Goes to Washington" remembers how that worked. Well, that got changed along the way and now all the opposition minority leader must do is inform the majority leader that his party is filibustering the bill and nothing happens until he decides to lift the filibuster. If he does not lift it, the proposed bill dies when that congress completes its two year term. No one has to make a speech or do anything else. Remember the 300 plus bills the House passed that were filibustered in the Senate? Well using the filibuster strategy the Republican Party stopped the Obama administration in its efforts to fulfill its promises that the people elected them to implement in all but a few instances; and even then, using only the THREAT of a filibuster, those few, like Obama Care, were severely altered versions of the original bills passed in the House. This was not the original intent of the Filibuster and it does not work in the best interests of the country and its citizens. As used today, it effectively changes the constitutional requirement of "majority rules" to the 3/5 rules or 60 votes out of a possible 100. And it is done without amending the Constitution!

Now we have another congress that wants to stop the Administration and this time the Republicans have the majority in the House. With the two very different ideologies it is unlikely much will be accomplished, but the conservative Republican's headed by efforts of the Tea Party congressmen, would not approve a new, higher debt ceiling instead using it as a THREAT to stop the administration budget and force its version through the Senate. Later they intend to use it as blackmail to gain the presidents signature on their previously House passed Ryan Republican budget. Tea Party members were adamant about getting their way and only effective last minute effort prevented that from occurring.

Whether we are Democrats, Independents or Republicans we need to look at all the issues and see what we want to support. I believe we should do what's important for our country with the first priority being job creation. This is not a party issue but an American issue and ideology should have no place in the decision. Remember the accumulated national debt is historic and represents what previous administrations have done in managing our country. The 2012 budget looks forward and is our future. We need to do what's best for our country and our children who will inherit the total results of our actions both financial and social; and we need to make this our first priority, not debt reduction. When we have full employment the relative size of the national debt will be reduced and when enough of our problems are resolved we can reduce the absolute size of the debt just as President Clinton did in the 1990s. So let's get our priorities straight and our number 1 item is Jobs!

The Ideology Argument

The mid-term elections in November 2010 resulted in the Republican Party gaining seats in both houses of congress. They gained enough for control of the House of Representatives but not enough for control of the Senate. Their leadership, Speaker Boehner and Senate minority leader McConnell, immediately interpreted this as a mandate from the people to implement their conservative agenda and ideology expressed by the Ryan budget and in essence have said we the people want domestic spending programs that support government services, education, health care and entitlements reduced or eliminated because we want smaller, more efficient government.

On the other hand, Democrats tell us that the election results were poor for them because the people were angry at President Obama because he did not keep his campaign promises. This was especially true of the very liberal left and independents. Democrat faithful say it was not Obama's fault it was because the Republicans refused to work collaboratively with Obama and stopped his programs to stimulate the economy, create more jobs, restructure and cost reduce healthcare and continue support of the aged, poor, children of the poor and lower middle class citing abuse of the Filibuster and extreme ideology as the problems. They further argue the Republicans want to reduce or eliminate everything from education programs to healthcare and take the money that is "saved" and give it the defense department and to the wealthy in the form of even greater tax cuts, even though it means extensive borrowing and increased national debt. Not only do they plan to make the Bush tax cuts permanent but will reduce the top income tax rate to 25%, 10% below the Bush plan top tax rates. And the Democrats claim that despite all of their arguments about the National debt and current deficit the Republicans make both current and future problems significantly worse and will not achieve a balanced budget until 2050.

The two parties could not be much further apart, so how do we determine whose ideology is closest to the right course of action for our country? Certainly we do not want to see the excellent progress we have made in class mobility and growth of a strong middle class to regress to pre 1930 levels. Nor do we want to return to the living standards, educational opportunities and individual rights status of that time. Nor do we want the aged, poor and temporarily down on their luck workers to lose their safety nets and life savings in bad economic periods; and most importantly, a financially weak or unstable country cannot possibly keep us on that track of excellence or protect us from enemies, So what de we ordinary citizens do?

How Did We Get Here?

Before we answer the question of what we should do let's start with a short review of the history that led us to our current dilemma. This impasse of ideologies didn't happen over night, it took a long time, over 75 years as a matter of fact. It has also gone through major adjustments at different times but in periods of national emergency in the past the parties have acted as one voice to support American needs and values. Over the years the Republican Party has increasingly become the party of the wealthy and big business while the Democratic Party has grown to be the party associated with minorities and the common people. Partly because the great social programs of the 20th century began under the Democrat Roosevelt and were continued by Democratic Presidents Truman, Kennedy, Johnson, Carter and Clinton the Democrats have been named "the tax and spend" party even though some of the lowest effective tax rates, greatest GDP growth and most balanced budgets occurred under their leadership.

It is also interesting to see how the meaning of labels has changed over the years. Originally the label "Conservative" or "Liberal" referred to how an individual interpreted the constitution. Was he a "strict" or "loose." constructionist" Now the labels refer to ideologies, spending and government size are only loosely related to fiscal management and interpretation of the constitution and are really more social conservative. In any event these labels are like talking points: they tell us very little and are frequently just simply rhetoric.

Ideologies and Their Effect on Budgets Deficits and Debt

We have talked in general a lot about ideologies and how the major parties differ but how do we interpret the impact of those differences on our economic and political systems? Is it important to us to know? I think it is because ideology has a great impact on how we approach governing our country; how we build our institutions and infrastructure; and, how we provide opportunity and assistance programs for our fellow citizens.

As mentioned earlier, the United States' approach to government prior to the early 20th century was "laissez faire", particularly the economy and social programs. This French phrase literally means to leave it alone and until Republican President Theodore Roosevelt went after the "robber barons" with his anti-trust legislation "laissez faire" was deemed the right way to manage our country's relationship to economic activity. No one thought the government should do much more than attempt to provide laws that protected big business. This anti-trust legislation was the first attempt to protect individuals and small business against big business by outlawing price fixing, corrupt trusts and unfair competition. It was about the extent of things the government became involved in until Franklin Roosevelt was elected in 1932.

When Roosevelt actually took office in the spring of 1933 it was in the midst of a worldwide depression. With a population a little over one hundred twenty million people the United States had more than 25 million unemployed workers; people were homeless living in crowded shelters, parks and hobo jungles with daily food needs filled by soup kitchens and bread lines where available through local charities. GDP growth was negative with banks failing daily, and bank failure in 1930 meant all deposits were lost. Roosevelt, a Democrat, took unprecedented action: he declared a bank holiday; instituted the Federal Deposit Insurance Corporation and worked with the Federal Reserve to develop a more positive and safer approach to management of the currency. As he progressed through his first term of office he instituted the Securities and Exchange Commission with broad regulatory powers over brokerage firms on Wall Street and introduced strong regulation of banks through the Federal Reserve. These regulations, strengthened by several presidents, remained in effect until George W Bush took office in 2001. Bush wiped out these most of these regulatory powers leading to the Real Estate over-valuation "bubble" which subsequently burst causing the Wall Street debacle of 2007-2009. The full result of this burst "bubble" with accompanying "derivatives" may not be known and understood for years.

Roosevelt also instituted Social Security Insurance and Unemployment Insurance and he initiated massive public works aimed at improving and, in some cases, creating infrastructure including highways, bridges; and, the massive rural electrification projects with dams located throughout the country. He initiated the Civilian Conservation Corps and expanded Conservation in general. He used the power of government to put the nation back to work and establish new direction for the citizenry. He took these actions because of his ideology, which simply stated was we as a nation have a basic responsibility to do for our citizens collectively what they cannot do for themselves individually, an ideology shared by Republican Abraham Lincoln, incidentally. In 1933 the citizens of this country were powerless to overcome the depression so government stepped in.

This worldwide depression exacerbated historical differences and elicited different responses in different countries. These different responses, which resulted eventually in World War 2, were: fascism in Italy, under Benito Mussolini Italy became a fascist nation directly controlling the production and economy; National Socialism in Germany which became a socialist total dictatorship under Adolph Hitler; and communism which under Stalin was a total and vicious dictatorship where the state owned the factors of production. All three countries instituted massive public works and built large armies which they used aggressively. Russia ended up allying itself with the Western powers in stopping Germany and Italy in the ensuing world war. The ideologies of all three differed from Roosevelt's, however: they saw their federal power as a way to expand the economic well being for their country and its citizens through conquest; Roosevelt saw using that power as a partnership of capitalism and state to help the citizens of our country by providing short-term and long-term jobs; developing infrastructure funded by deficit spending and supported by a new set of economic rules and safety nets to help individuals improve and protect their economic efforts. Different ideologies produced different approaches to governing and economics.

The fact that Franklin Roosevelt was a Democrat doesn't mean Democrats are somehow better than Republicans. Remember Lincoln, a Republican, shared the same attitudes as Roosevelt when questioned about his ideology and most experts believe that, if he had lived, reconstruction under Lincoln would have been far gentler and more generous and effective in healing and bringing the country together than methods supported Andrew Johnson. And remember, the whole concept of government regulation was initiated under Theodore Roosevelt, a Republican. Harry Truman, a Democrat, gave us the GI bill, rebuilt Europe with the Marshall Plan and made major changes in the rights of unions and management. Dwight Eisenhower, a Republican gave us the Interstate Highway system and the initial space programs; Democrat Jack Kennedy initiated the moon/space program that gave us the incredible technological strength and world leadership that we have today that came from it; and Lyndon Johnson, a Southern Democrat, gave us the Great Society and the landmark Civil Rights laws of the 1960s. Reagan broke the Russian will and bank account and won the cold war. The "tax and spend" Democrat president, Bill Clinton, gave us enormous prosperity, balanced budgets and debt reduction and created an incredible 23 million new jobs during his eight years in office. All of these presidents exhibited a strong sense of caring about the people and future of the country and all but one added significantly to the national debt but only two of them produced balanced budgets: one was a Republican, Dwight Eisenhower; and, one was a Democrat, Bill Clinton.

Since the Bush 2 administration, 2001-2009, we have seen a progressively more hostile form of politics driven by increasingly opposing ideologies of the major parties, augmented by irresponsible radicals in both parties and exacerbated by equally biased and irresponsible talk shows and news commentary that has inflamed an already angry populace. Under that administration we saw the beginning of 2 wars; deregulation of banks and Wall Street causing the financial collapse of the real estate and real estate bond markets in 2007; and the ensuing Great Recession starting in 2007 which still plagues us. The total effect on our economy is yet to be fully determined but the National Debt has increased from the approximate $5.6 trillion in 2001 to over $15 trillion today and we are still adding to that with annual deficits of over $1 trillion and unemployment officially still at 8.5% which in reality is perhaps twice that.

Politicians argue about which president did what but it is clear that the bulk of the problem is attributable to the actions of Bush 2. Remember in addition to the wars, huge tax reductions and resulting GDP stagnation, he also initiated an unbudgeted $850 billion bail-out of Wall Street in November of 2008 which fell into Obama's 2009 appropriation budget which started on October 1, 2008. He planned the fiscal 2009 budget that was inherited by Obama, who took office in January 2009. In addition, 3 months after taking office Obama went back to congress for $830 billion more to finish the inadequate Bush Wall Street bail-out, which was far worse than the Bush administration calculated. Obama also used these deficits to save the auto industry and an estimated 7 million jobs. An even more important contributor to the "Great Recession" was the failure of the Bush Administration to create jobs, only about 1 million net jobs were created during the eight years he was in office officially leaving about. 14 million people unemployed, or about 9.5% of the work force in our country. Experts say unemployment was twice that level.

So that brings us to the present. We now have Republican Party with an ideology very different from the party of Eisenhower or even Reagan or Bush 1. The Democrats have also changed from the party of Kennedy and Johnson and are made up of extremely liberal ideologists on the left and more conservative moderates in the center with a few "blue dogs" on the right. More importantly more people today classify themselves as independents which in many ways I believe is good for our country. When you add the ideologies of the extreme right wing of the Republican Party and the myriad of talking heads to the equation we have so much ideological noise it is really hard to find the truth. Remember we are after what's best for the United States of America, ourselves and our families. So with all this background information where do we start?

CHAPTER 7

Dealing With Ideology and Political Parties

T he problem is that all of us contribute to the problem. We all have our strong beliefs and preferences. We all have our ideologies that in most cases are tempered by our reasonable natures and simple common courtesy. But when they are not under control we become guilty of attempting to force our beliefs and prejudices on our fellow citizens, too. Our form of government allows for such differences and offers us a route to finding solutions to these differences through debate and the rule of law initiated and implemented through our elected representatives and our courts. Fundamental to our system is the concept that majority rules; and fundamental to all these is the concept of collaboration to find the best solution for the country as a whole without infringing on the basic contract we citizens have with the United States, the Constitution of the United States.

Implicit in our communications with our representatives and those who would be our representatives is open, complete honesty. Likewise we have the right to expect the same from the media reporting on events involving the people's business and our representatives. Ideally this communication would also be free of prejudice and bias. Alas! This is not always what we get and in the case of talk shows we almost never get it. That is why it is so important that we strive to understand what is being said and what it means to us and our country. So what can we do?

The Effect of Political Parties

Various ideologies have different and sometimes multiple sources. Some come from religious beliefs and training; some from strong beliefs regarding individual freedoms and that each person should be responsible for himself not relying on government help. Others believe we must be strong economically and frugal; some not just strong economically and militarily but a super power ready to police and re-organize the world. While all of these beliefs may be important some are in direct conflict. To consolidate an out of balance political philosophy and approach to government based on an extreme ideology opposed by large numbers of other people creates polarization between groups. When these groups exert their political influence to shift party approach to government to force their ideology on the rest of the nation we have a very dangerous situation if enough common ground for collaborative effort cannot be found. This is where we find ourselves today.

Our major parties, Democrat and Republican, control most of the seats in Congress and, when either has the majority over the other, that party controls legislation including budgets, appointments of federal judges and approval of cabinet members and other senior officials. Historically, the founding fathers opposed political parties. They believed the forums of the House of Representatives and the oversight of the Senate allowed all relevant opinions to be presented, debated and resolved. But from day one major ideological differences regarding states rights and slavery caused them to seek strength through unity and that pushed them into parties. Without going into the evolution of the original parties to those we have today it is enough to know that changes occurred within each original party. Old parties died and gave birth to new ones as new ideas were born by individuals, accepted by groups and incorporated into political action spawning new national goals. Since the rise of the Republican Party in the nineteenth century numerous third party movements have come and gone. Some just died out but some of their ideas were at least partially absorbed into either the Democratic of Republican Parties. The important thing is that parties have been self regulating internally and changed as the country changed and as the will of their leaders and constituents changed.

The two major parties we have today have continued to undergo change. The Democratic Party basically controlled the south from the civil war until the 1970s. After Lyndon Johnson, a southern Democrat, forced the civil rights legislation of 1966 into law, the southern states moved en mass to the Republican Party and the "solid south (Democratic)" became the "solid south (Republican)". This change in party control of the south was a result of changes within the country driven by special interests groups that insisted in equality for all being resisted by a region of the United States wanting to continue the restrictive "separate but equal" restrictions that were born of a horrible civil war reconstruction period and existed until addressed by Johnson. A good thing in terms of morality and law but the

Republican Party that emerged was quite different. It had been identified with big business for over 100 years but now began identifying itself by a new name "Conservative". As mentioned earlier, the original meaning of the word "conservative" had to do with how one interpreted the constitution, particularly in terms of states rights and federalism. In the 21st century it really refers to a number of other things as well: few government provided social services and less police, fire and environmental protection with the emphasis on much smaller government and financial austerity are the key rallying points. But several that are also included are based on religious and special interest group demands such as liberal gun laws, outlawing abortion, same sex marriage and no military service by homosexuals. They also have weak civil rights objectives.

In a sense this is a form of strict constructionism but it is also the demands of the few to control the values and life practices of the many through political control. Does the religious right have the right to force these "moral" issues as they see them on our society as a whole? Do 2nd amendment supporters have the right to interpret the constitution as they do and force their views on guns, particularly automatic weapons, into law? Do homosexuals have the same civil rights as the rest of the population, the constitution does not address the issue? These are questions that must be answered by all of us. We need to see the issues clearly and vote our consciences. The arguments of the left and right are distorted by prejudice and other rhetoric and we need to get through that to the truth.

Unfortunately we do not find the clear unbiased analyses of these issues in the political parties. It's a little like trying to grow delicate flowers. If the weeds get too entrenched and are allowed to choke off the nutrients and block the sunlight the flowers die. If the weeds are eliminated the flowers have a chance to flourish. For years we have looked to political parties to manage our political "weeds", the lies, distortions and rhetoric sent out by special interests groups. Until the Bush administration they have always managed to rally at critical points in our history and pull together for the good of the country. It is much different today, our politics are polarized and collaboration is dead in Washington because of totally different agendas of the major parties. Communications have also changed. The ownership of wealth in the United States which had been slowly shifting to the super rich for over twenty years, dramatically increased under Bush and the large corporations and the wealthy top 2% of the nation now control approximately 80% of the total wealth of the country. They now have the money to create, package and deliver any message they choose and they bombard us with their carefully crafted "talking points" like the Tea Party "taking back their country" and "cutting back spending". They offer no valid factual support and when challenged for factual support instead answer questions with more "talking points", like "the democrats' spending is out of control". They neglect to mention who put the bulk of the national debt on the books and who authored the 2009 budget let alone to factually address the huge financial problems that carried over to 2010 and 2011 because of the Wall Street Debacle and resulting Great Recession caused by those eight years of wars and ridiculous tax cuts.

Even though the Bush Republican administration is responsible for our current dilemma they must equally share the blame with a complacent, do-nothing Democratic Party. They sat by and allowed these tax cuts and wars to happen. The did not challenge deregulation of the banks and Wall Street and even in the years when they controlled both houses of Congress they did not reverse the Bush actions of the previous years and again stood idly by while the Senate Republican minority, under minority leader Mitch McConnell totally stopped them from enacting any meaningful legislation. No our problems involve both parties, the leadership of both parties and the system that perpetuates their self-serving separate agenda approach to representing us. They do not do the people's business, they due the business of the rich and powerful.

The historical controls that limited such spending have been largely eliminated by a Supreme Court that has chosen to legislate their political will from the bench and are supportive of the organized efforts of the super rich and corporations to control political thinking. We have the internet, but while everyone has access to it only some read the information presented there and for the most part only the social blogs. We need an organized method of fighting for the things we believe in and the only available organizations that have the clout to name candidates and deliver coherent messages are the Political Parties. So what do we do with this conundrum?

Taking a Lesson from the Rich and Powerful

We are facing a well financed adversary intent on distribution of wealth and political power to the already rich and powerful and if they are successful we will see the middle class disappear in this country and that would be a tragedy. This is not about our current parties solving the problems. Our current parties have lost the ability to do that because of the similarity of the parties: they both seek power to control, not the responsibility to do the business of the citizens of our country in their best interests. Oh they talk about their philosophies and point out various achievements but, keep in mind, those achievements are history. What have they done recently? For the most part they have supported the rich and powerful and have been rewarded with money power and prestige. Watch what they do, not what they say. When the Republican's spout their dedication to balanced budgets and debt reduction ask yourself, "where were they in 2003 and 2004 when the wars and tax cuts happened and the banks and Wall Street were deregulated; and for that matter 2007, 2008 and 2009 when Wall Street imploded and triggered the great Recession and the taxpayers, you and I, had to bail them out?

This is political expediency. Why political expediency? Look at what they want to cut. It's the smallest part of the budget and it does not impact their benefactors, the rich and powerful. It attacks the poor and weak, those who do not contribute to political campaigns and who do not hire lobbyists and have no means to retaliate. How sincere are these cuts? And the Democrats who sit idly by and allow the poor and weak to be harmed while extending tax reductions and other concessions to the rich and powerful that are many times larger than what is taken from the poor and weak. What makes this so absurd is they now want more from ordinary citizens like you and I so they can cut taxes on the rich and powerful even more and they are willing to borrow and increase the nation's debt to accomplish that. This is not conjecture! The House of Representatives passed this proposed 2012 budget in April of 2011 and are now attempting to find a way to make it legal by forcing the Democratic Senate to pass it. How do they expect to accomplish this feat? Simple, at first they used the threat of not extending the debt ceiling which, under law, will prevent the government from spending in excess of the current debt ceiling making the United States of America technically bankrupt. So all federal employees including Medicare and Social Security and US security debt holders would not be paid, at least not on time. Next time the threat will be approval of the 2012, or 2013 budget or the debt ceiling increase.

So what can we learn from all this? Well, it's pretty simple: once we learn to decipher what these icons are telling us; what they stand for and what it is we stand for and what we want; we start by voting for candidates that support what we support. At the same time take a lesson from the rich and powerful to change the political parties so they represent our goals and that means we participate and debate issues within the parties, at town hall meetings, at the caucuses and re-shape the parties from the bottom up. Drive out the party bosses by uniting, developing your own talking points (supported by facts) and change the parties from the inside. It will take too long, you say? The current crop of people running the parties have worked at it for years relying on just that kind of complacency to make them the winners, the king-makers, as it were. Remember, the old adage is," United We Stand, Divided We Fall". At this point we are on the way to our knees. If we delay longer we'll be flat on our backs. So forget which party you do or don't belong to or support, learn to hear and understand what they are saying and doing; vote for the candidate that supports your views; bond together with those that share your views and make the leadership of the parties and government aware of what you are doing. Look what the Tea Party did in one short election cycle and they brought nothing but their special interests and talking points to the people. But they packaged those special interests, wrapped them in the flag and sold them with Patriotic "talking points" based on little if any facts and benefiting no one but themselves and the rich and powerful, like the Koch brothers who funded them.

CHAPTER 8

Who Are We?

Growing up during the great depression was quite different than today. We were the generation sandwiched between two World Wars and just entering the technology world we have around us today. We had automobiles, but we also had horse drawn icemen and milkmen and who could ever forget the horse drawn ice cream man and junkman? Electric street cars and buses roamed the streets of Los Angeles. There was no TV but radio filled our needs with Jack Armstrong, Captain Midnight and the Green Hornet and for the old folks it was Lux Radio Theater and Jack Benny. Everyone who could find a job worked, we all contributed to the family needs and that included the kids; I mowed lawns and delivered papers and when I was short the 10 cents for the Saturday matinee, I collected bottles from neighbors and returned them for the deposit at the corner store. We were proud to be self-supporting and fairness and honesty were practiced and admired by the very diverse community in general. Franklin Roosevelt was president and we all supported him and his efforts as he led us out of the Depression and through World War 2 and into the prosperity and the new technical world the followed.

As I look back I now can clearly see that my basic values were formed during those years. I think that was true for most of us of that generation as well. We worked hard, didn't have a lot of material things and didn't think much about them. My parents stressed education as did most parents of the kids in my class. I went through graduate school and a Master's degree and of the 42 students in my eighth grade catholic school class, located in the heart of southwest Los Angeles, two-thirds went on to college.

We also got real life lessons in helping our fellow man. My mother's sisters and their husbands and my grandmother all moved in and lived with us during the war and all were active in different war and charitable programs in addition to their day jobs. We donated to charities and brought food to neighbors down on their luck. No one had much but we shared what we did have. I think what was happening with Roosevelt's social programs instilled the idea that we had to stick together and that idea remained with us as a group through all the trauma and turmoil of post war America. To this day we have a fundamental mind set that the poor and weak should be helped to help themselves and that all of us have value as human beings. I view these values as fundamental to life and have seen them expressed by Democrats and Republicans throughout my life. These values are universal, not party related and we embrace them as individuals not party members.

How far we have come

Unfortunately we have evolved away from that spirit of generosity and caring I saw during my life. It didn't happen all at once but gradually little by little and today we can se just how far we have come when we hear our leaders propose we balance our budget and cure our deficit woes by taking away programs which the poor and needy depend on. We see them attempting to pass budgets in the middle of the worst recession since the great depression that cut social programs, government stimulus spending, programs to re-build our infrastructure and programs to invest in our competitive future. Where is the positive thinking of Roosevelt, Eisenhower, Kennedy, Reagan and Clinton? Where are the infrastructure programs that built dams, electrified the nation and provided the greatest highway structure in the world? Where is the optimism of the moon program that made us number one in the hi-tech world, and where is the courage that forced the Russians to "tear down that wall" by out spending them and doing it by deficit financing and accumulation of national debt? All of a sudden it is all about money and all about fear: fear of not being able to afford to be the greatest nation in the world. We didn't get here by being afraid. We faced our threats, solved our problems and drove ahead and won. We took what generations of Americans built and made it better—made our country stronger. Now, a large part of our political leadership wants to sell us out because their personal and political agendas don't call for sacrifice. Sacrifice would mean they might not make that next million or billion or whatever it is they want. The fact is they do not want to do the people's business, they want to use the power we gave them to do what's best for America to feather their own nests.

Some of you are probably saying, oh, you just want to push a political agenda." Let's go back to the earlier chapters on how the economy works and talk a little about what's really going on.

Remember the whole purpose of this book is for you to become an informed citizen to develop your own strategy and support those that share your vision and priorities. I am certainly not suggesting you adopt the Democrats, Republicans', Libertarians' or even my views. What we are striving for is truth and what's best for America. Let's look at the major issues as enlightened economists might.

The Current Issues

The United States has a process for budget approval that requires the administration to submit a budget proposal to Congress for approval. In the late spring of 2011 we found ourselves in a difficult position. The administration had delivered the 2012 proposed Budget to Congress. The Speaker of the House of Representatives had rejected that and accepted a budget proposal by Representative Paul Ryan, Chairman of the House Budget committee. It had been passed in the House and rejected by the Senate. We now had no approved budget for 2012. To complicate matters further the 2011 budget passed at the last moment in 2010 would produce approximately a $1.4 trillion deficit for 2011. The current approved national debt was approximately $14.3 trillion and we had technically exceeded that per the approved 2011 budget: the debt ceiling must be raised or expenditures reduced or the United States will be unable to meet its obligations to employees, vendors and debt holders.

At this point the Republican Speaker, John Boener and congressman Ryan proposed spending reductions of about $90 billion, and under threat of shutting down the federal government the President agreed. These budget cuts will reduce government employment and reduce services to the poor, women's health programs and welfare. Speaker Boener and his party have stated they will increase spending by one dollar for every one dollar cut from existing spending programs as their basis of future budget negotiations and simultaneously stated he will not consider increase taxes on the super wealthy. This is the outlook for 2012 budget approval by the House. We are at an impasse; what should our leaders do?

Setting political rhetoric aside what should we consider? Is debt reduction our top priority or with 14 million or more Americans still unemployed or should job creation be most important? No question we would all feel more comfortable if the debt was where Clinton left it in 2001, but Bush changed all that and the reality is, it is high. Is it too high for safety? Some say yes, some say no. Who's right? How do we assess the risk? And how does the recession, inflation and GDP growth enter into the calculation? We have a lot of questions and, judging from what is coming out of Washington, not many answers. So where do we start?

Maybe the best place to start is with more questions: Can we fix the debt problem by cutting spending programs which reduces jobs; cutting spending that stimulates new job formation and levying no new taxes on the rich and still produce enough new jobs to employ our working population?

Let's take it analytically. When we reduce jobs two things happen immediately and some other things happen later. The first thing is middle and low income salaries have negative savings rates so the lost pay which is probably 70% of the spending cut will not be spent in the consumption part of GDP. The second thing that occurs is that the people who lose their jobs will draw unemployment. So the cuts reduce government jobs which reduces consumption and tax revenue, increases government spending for unemployment and since that is less than the normal pay rate the net effect is almost a dollar for dollar offset. No real improvement but GDP starts down as those unemployed reduce spending. Later when unemployment compensation runs out consumption really drops and so do tax revenues. Remember the other things I mentioned? They are the fan-out events that money unspent produces, the multiplier in reverse: the incomes of the dry cleaner, the butcher the baker all decline and more jobs are lost, and less consumption results in more of the same—fewer jobs, less consumption and less tax revenue. The CBO does not see a balanced budget using the bill passed by the House until around 2050 and a cumulative deficit by 2023 of more than $5 trillion more than today.

Is spending reduction the way out for us? Well so far the net financial affect is negative, jobs are lost, GDP is down and tax revenues are down. It is the stuff that recessions are made of, not what recoveries look like.

What about increasing taxes on the super rich, say everyone with adjusted gross incomes above $250,000? The Congressional Budget Office, (CBO) says it will produce close to $300 billion a year in revenue; the House leadership says it will cost jobs. They claim reducing those taxes will create jobs. What does history tell us? Clinton raised taxes to the identical rate currently proposed by the Democrats in the 1990's and 23million jobs were created, the budget was balanced and national debt was retired. Bush reduced taxes in 2003 to where they are now and had only a net increase of 1 million jobs in the eight years he was president. What's more he more than doubled, some say tripled, the national debt; left us in the worst financial condition since1930 and created the Wall Street debacle through deregulation of the banks.

Sounds like history supports a tax increase for the wealthy.

The administration budget proposal contains provisions for continuing with the programs supporting the poor and needy; provisions for reducing military spending; provisions for re-building the infrastructure of roads, bridges and other public works and most importantly, provisions for investing in "Green Technology" to position the United States at the forefront of the development of this major new market. His approach doesn't contain much other job stimulus but these offer the opportunity to create approximately 5 million plus and with fan-out probably millions more. The CBO has looked at the probable results and although it does not produce a balanced budget until 2024, it builds debt at a slower rate and produces millions more jobs while rebuilding the country and is still aggressively helping the poor, the senior citizen community and preserving Medicare and Medicaid.

Is this aggressive enough? I ask myself if Eisenhower, Kennedy, Roosevelt or Reagan would say it was and I get the strong feeling they would not like this path, it is too weak. It's not what would have won WW 2; it's not the moon program; and not even close to the Clinton/Gingrich collaboration of the 90s. No, it's too conservative to effect rapid recovery but it does eventually get us back to some reasonable level of growth, if we forget about the millions who will remain unemployed and the loss of middle class jobs to emerging economies.

The Solution

The most difficult thing for me to accept is that we are debating the wrong solutions. The House Budget is unacceptable to me, not because it was authored and passed by the Republicans in power but because it takes nothing into consideration but cutting programs to save wealth with no careful thought regarding what that really means. And they have nothing to say about adding and building to create wealth. What good is a wealthy treasury if it is not working for us? What good is life without dreams and aspirations? What good is life when we are full of fear? No the Republican plan is a long list of the wrong things to do.

The administration plan is too timid because they fear the Republican, Tea Party dominated resistance to any spending proposals and thus it doesn't go far enough with any of the proposals. It is in the right direction but it is weak and timid. Where is the spirit and toughness of Lyndon Johnson when he took on his OWN party PLUS the Republicans and passed the civil rights laws of the 60's? We need leaders with dedication to what is best for America who also have the courage to fight for the opportunities to keep us a great country: one that supports a strong middle class; encourages class mobility; educates its citizens to take advantage of that mobility and invests in the future for all of us. In my opinion now is not the time to run for cover. We are the strongest, most admired country this earth has seen to date. Our credit rating is still good. We are not in danger of bankruptcy unless we forget what made us great and follow the advice of those with different agendas other than what's best for America. So what's the solution?

We need bold *collaborative* leadership to structure the plans and programs to take us forward. Collaborative, not bi-partisan, because the term bi-partisan is nothing more than a fancy word for political compromise. There should be no politics in job creation, no special interests and credit for solving the problem should be co-equal. The most singularly important problem facing us today is unemployment and we need the infrastructure and Green programs of President Obama and we need the collaborative efforts of both parties to plan and implement them plus the participation of the corporate world. If we really want to cut costs let's go after the pork projects and the abuse of the major Medicare and Social Security programs and their long term existence and fix them forever by taxing the whole stream of income. And most importantly, we must raise taxes on the super wealthy, if we do not they will simply hoard the money and not create jobs. History has clearly shown us there is no "trickle down" effect. However they will invest in job creation to increase their wealth rather than pay those taxes so it's a win/win deal for us as a nation: if they pay we get the revenues; if they invest to get the tax exemption, we get the jobs. And let's make our elected leaders respond by burying them with letters and in the final analysis threaten them with losing their jobs if they don't start doing the peoples' business as we the people see it!

If you don't like my analysis do your own. All I ask is leave your political loyalties at the door. We need objective reasoning and solutions that work.

CHAPTER 9

What are "They" really Saying?

O k, we've talked about some of the tricks people use to avoid complete disclosure and push their own agendas; we've talked about some basic economic facts and principles; how people control messages and thinking and the budget and congress. Now let's get into what "they" are saying—what "they" are really saying.

So much of what we get from politicians and the media is in the form non-stop repetition of talking points and labels that we tend to stop listening and start accepting what they are saying, or I should say seem to be saying. We accept what they say, not on the basis of logic, not as good and true ideas but because they relentlessly pound their messages through captive media, and because of our outdated party loyalties and/or our likes and dislikes of individuals we have never met. We also impute characteristics into our leaders and give them nicknames like McCain is a "Straight Talker", (Could that have come from the sign he had painted on his campaign bus?); or "Obamacare" is a government takeover inferring there is something bad about the program and by inference make it reflect "badly" on the president.

We form opinions of these political leaders without conscious cognitive consideration of the talking points, simply responding to the hard sell tactics of parties repeating the message over and over. Have we considered what the Tea party is all about? Does it represent a truly patriotic grass roots movement or is it a clever ruse financed by the rich to help them get what they want? If we learn to listen by also watching carefully and observing what they actually do we can make a logical analysis and reach a logical conclusion. Analyzing what their proposals actually produce for our country and listening to unbiased third party factually based opinions will give us a much better chance of arriving at the correct choice for candidates for office and which proposals to support or to reject. This will put you back in the driver's seat and the politicians will become real public servants.

Let's look at a few current issues. The big one is the economic recovery and how to stimulate it. We talked previously about the approaches of the major parties and what the independent analysts at CBO concluded. Now let's talk about why they reached their conclusions. To begin with CBO treats each proposal in light of current law and how the proposed legislation changes things from that perspective. Their analysis does not include the actions that MAY follow, so unless the proposal is sufficiently detailed to provide solid information on which to base a forecast, their forecasts tend to be conservative. Hears how the CBO sees things currently:

The Ryan budget proposal hinges on two basic claims:

1. That cutting spending for support and welfare programs will

a. Significantly reduce deficit spending and reduce the national debt while positively impacting job creation. And,

b. Keeping the Bush tax cuts in place for the wealthy and then reducing them even more in the future will stimulate the economy and increase jobs now and in the future.

In other words "they", in this case Ryan, and the Republicans, are telling us that if we implement programs that give more to the rich who don't spend or invest the savings; and if we reduce disposable income for the poor, senior citizens and disabled who spend everything they receive on goods and services that demand will increase and drive GDP causing new investment and jobs creation. OK, what does traditional economic theory and history tell us about those assumptions? Exactly the opposite, read Chapter 2 again. If total demand goes down GDP goes down. Hoover tried that in 1929 when he refused to get involved with the economic crash and we had the great depression. Bush, coupled with his tax cuts and privatization, tried that in 2003 through 2009. The result was we lost jobs as a percent of the total and unemployment went from 6% to 10.5%. Plus in this case the Ryan proposal also penalizes the weak and powerless. What do we do with them when their safety nets are removed? And if the rest of the vague plan is implemented the CBO tells us that we will see government tax revenues decline by about an additional 30% and GDP to drift downward with increasing unemployment and the National debt to grow to over $25 trillion in 10 years or less. Remember the CBO is not a partisan group. They exist as a group of professionals to advise congress and government on the probable outcome of proposed legislation.

What about President Obama's budget proposal? Well it generally meets the economic and history tests. Roosevelt, Truman. Eisenhower, Kennedy, Johnson, Nixon, Ford, Carter, Reagan. Bush 1 and Clinton all followed the same path and when Bush 2 took over he had a $200 billion surplus and a national debt of approximately $5.5 trillion. His policies left us with $14 trillion in debt, a declining economy in recession and unemployment of over 10% when he left office in 2009. In fact, Clinton raised taxes on the wealthy, created a balanced budget and created 23 million jobs during his 8 years in office.

I recently read an article written by a nationally syndicated columnist criticizing President Obama as stuck in outdated 20th century Keynesian economic policies while the Republican/Ryan approach represented brilliant *21st century economic* thinking. History tells us the 20th century economic policies, regardless of problems produced a thriving economy, the richest, most powerful, and most admired country the world has ever seen. On the other hand the 21st century approach of Bush et al has produced wars, chaos, conflict among our citizens on a scale never before experienced and massive wealth transfer to the already rich and powerful.

If the Ryan budget does not stimulate GDP and does not create jobs and economic theory and history tell us it is exactly the wrong course of action, why would we want it regardless of party? Why does the radical right want government spending and taxes to be lower as their first priority? What is the real impact of our large National debt and who actually holds it?

Let's go back and analyze what "they" are telling us. Our reason for electing these people to congress and the presidency in Washington is for them to represent us; that is, they exist only to do the peoples' business not their own. Our view of doing the peoples' business is that "they" should fix the sick economy and provide jobs and "they" see it as going back to the failed policies of Hoover and Bush. Maybe we should be looking at what their real agenda is since "they" are not interested in doing what we think is necessary maybe history will help us understand what "they" are really hoping to achieve.

I recently heard Bernie Saunders, Independent Senator from Vermont and avowed Socialist, offer some factual details that help us understand what "they" have managed to accomplish since the Reagan administration. The beauty of Bernie Saunders is he owes no allegiance to either major party. His staff did an analysis of who controls the wealth in our country as a function of income and how it has shifted since Reagan took office. According to Mr. Saunders the richest 4% in the US own 80% of the assets of the country up from the top 4% owning 60% in 1980. Further the top group accounted for about 80% of the income growth during the same period and wage earners, the so-called middle class, went down in asset ownership and saw their incomes stay relatively flat while prices increased.

The Ryan budget would potentially continue the trend of shrinking the middle class while putting more and more financial control in the hands of the rich. Couple these probabilities with

Supreme Court actions like the "Citizens United" decision allowing corporations to contribute unlimited funds to political campaigns and the "Wal-Mart" class action decision virtually eliminating the class action law suit and the ability of the middle class to defend itself is further weakened as are their positions in collective bargaining and elections.

So what are "they" saying? Some see it as an obvious con job to manipulate us to support our own political and economic destructive re-structuring. Their success depends on the common voter identifying with the idea he will also be rich in the future and as such will buy into the programs they are pushing in Congress. In fact these programs will continue to shrink the middle class, reduce class mobility and eventually make it much more difficult to attain wealth by severely restricting economic opportunity. If allowed to succeed I see it eventually affecting all areas of our lives from birth through senility for this is only one more of a long progression of political actions emanating from Washington and some Republican controlled state governments.

There will many more, further restricting opportunities reducing government services before this ill informed group is through. Their obvious outcome and their inferred goal is to create a two class society made up of the very rich and powerful at the top and the poor and weak at the bottom. It sounds like medieval Europe or Japan of the Samurais, not the United States of America in the 21st century.

The marketing package currently being used to sell us on these suicidal programs is interesting. "They" are in the process of totally turning around from being the big spenders of the early

2000 s to the watchdogs of government spending of the 2010 s and now are fanatically concerned with the large debt and high government spending. "They" frantically wave their arms and blame everything on Obama. I am speaking of both parties. The Democrats have rolled over and become completely docile, opposing nothing and blaming Bush; and the Democrats and Republicans blame Obama and his dreaded Obamacare which has had little if any effect on the deficit and debt. One of the major changes made by Obama has been placing the real costs of the two wars in the budget which is over $200 billion a year and during the peak of the Iraq war over $400 billion and it was primarily funded through separate, off-budget special appropriations by Bush. Their irrational concern for the debt now is virtually insane. Like all debt it represents the total effect of PRIOR actions measured in dollars. It will grow if we cannot manage current GDP, that's what controls the whole problem, and shrink if we do manage it successfully and have a tax policy that provides sufficient revenues.

The National debt of some $14.5 trillion is owed both to government debtors, mainly Social security, and to other domestic investors with about 60% or $10 trillion to outsiders. If we deal with both Social Security and Medicare by stopping abuse and fraud, developing a new Social Security actuarial model and extending the tax to all income to support the new model they will be solvent and we can deal with the external debt by managing the rest of our economy more effectively and efficiently. The best way to do that is to maximize all federal revenue that does not impact consumption: increase the tax on the rich and cut all pork barrel projects that do not increase consumption. Thirdly eliminate fraud in all the programs. The amount of the debt is not unreasonable especially considering the comparative international situation.

That brings us back to the major issue. The problem is GDP and the issue holding that up is consumption and behind that is jobs. We need to focus on how jobs are created and find out what is not happening that needs to happen. The entire Ryan Budget Is focused on other objectives and the Obama budget does far too little and none of it is soon enough. We need immediate action and that will include income support extensions for unemployment and convincing the financial community to loan money to small businesses. For that lending to occur Bankers need evidence the United states has an economic policy of growth and one that both major parties support. One party holding the other hostage for election advantages is NOT doing the "Peoples' Business"

In summary we need our elected officials to understand the messages we are getting are not acceptable. We expect our elected representatives to do our business not theirs and we need jobs, not rhetoric about cutting spending and the debt. We want action that impacts NOW not in one, two or ten years. Stop using scare tactics only meant to manipulate people and start giving us definitive, clear programs for economic recovery or we'll get a complete new team in Washington, congress and administration, regardless of how much money their benefactors spend trying to elect their lackeys.

CHAPTER 10

The Purpose of Political Parties

The political party history has been one of evolution since the founding of the country.

"The two original national parties were the Federalist Party and the Democratic-Republican Party. In 1816, the Federalist Party died out leaving a single political party for a short time. However, a split in the Democratic-Republican Party in the mid-1820s gave rise two factions: the National Republicans and the Democrats. When Andrew Jackson lost in 1824, Jackson's supporters created their own organization to get him elected. After his election in 1828, that organization became known as the Democratic Party."

(Source: By Martin Kelly, About.com)

So the surviving party was the GOP, The Grand Old Party of the Republicans. The Federalists, the original party dominated by Alexander Hamilton disappeared. When the Federalists ceased to exist, the Democrat-Republican party became the origin of the two major parties of today. They didn't get here without turmoil and lots of change, however, and over the years have switched sides on many, many, issues including social programs, states rights and slavery and even the meaning of the terms liberal and conservative. Some of these changes were a result of changing social and economic times; some due to cataclysmic events like the civil war and economic panics; and some due to new parties formed to effect social changes. The parties survived because they assimilated these ideas into their platforms. What is important is that they changed because of the action of citizens like you and I. Blind party loyalty would have resulted in the death of one or both parties, so the two parties changed in order to survive. As I look at the major parties today I see the evolution has taken a couple of bad turns and none offer an approach to government that I believe is necessary to provide the kind of successful management of our country that will enable us to effectively compete in the next phase of our development; and, if we do not make the changes necessary we will become just like other great powers in history—history. The dream we all share will not be fulfilled and may in fact become a nightmare. I attribute this abysmal condition to leadership with their own agendas; they are not in office to do the peoples' business, they are out to feather their own nests and the political party is their enabler, with our help of course.

Most significant changes have been driven by strong social and economic demands. Even the civil war was in part caused by the economic issue of low cost labor through slavery. Although only a social issue to many citizens most historians claim it was the major States Rights issue of our history: the right of the individual states to make decisions regarding the issue of slavery and the rights of people of color. The parties at the time, Republicans in the North and Democrats in the

South looked to different interpretations of the constitution as validation for their actions: those in the South believed the 3/5s compromise defining representation in congress inferred they were right and since nothing specific was spelled out it was a states rights issue and not a Federal one. The North believed it was a Federal issue because the language that was used inferred the "3/5s" such individuals were citizens with rights guaranteed by the constitution. After the war the Republicans led the efforts for reconstruction in the South and forgiveness restoring full rights of the rebellious South and aiding with social programs. Since then other interests have come to dominate and shape the parties and now the Democratic Party is the party of social concern, responsibility and civil rights and the Republican Party the party of business, limited government and strong States Rights condemning government and wanting to eliminate all social responsibility of government.

So much for history, the major lesson is that political parties are responsive to what the political leadership sees as best for the nation and we the people should accept what they decide. This is a far cry from the freedom Jefferson et al saw for us over 200 years ago. It's even further from the things we have fought and died for over the last 200 years. It is the kind of benevolent servitude we relate to Medieval Europe with the Kings, Dukes and Princes at the top and poor tradesmen and serfs at the bottom. I don't like this model of the New United States that the 21st century economic policies of the Ryan led Republican Party offers. Nor do I like the spineless response of the Democratic Party and their counter proposal. We need to change not just one but both and to do that we need new party leadership. Unfortunately that requires we change the people at the top because they appoint the Party leaders. These are the same senators, congressmen and administration officials that are attempting to take us down the primrose path to a 21st century version of a medieval monarchy, where money is god and he with the most money, is King.

So what do we do?

Keep in mind the one thing, all of these officials respond to votes. We are the keys to their security. The problem is we need to work together and only then do we have a voice. Letters, emails blogs and phone calls are good. Attendance at Town hall meetings prepared to present questions and alternatives is better. But long term we have to get to party leaders and that means getting active in the political party of your choice where you can fight for what you believe is best for the country and form alliances with those with similar ideas. We need to make ourselves heard and the parties have the communication and control capabilities to take our message out to the people. Voting is mandatory but is our last line of defense, a chance to act as an individual and we *must* do that. Influencing the small group and then the larger and finally the total group multiplies the impact.

One of the problems we have today is the impact money makes on all elections. Much of the flow of money to both state and federal elections is through the parties. They work ceaselessly to raise money as do all the elected representatives in Congress. They know and work with the very wealthy and corporate donors and set the agenda regarding who gets elected and money is generally what gets the job done. Unfortunately, the price is the elected representative ends up having only one master and that master is the one supplying the money for his election.

The Tea party people tried the "grass roots" approach and used the tea party fable in colonial Boston as the rallying point of the group. When the professional politicians and financiers saw what was happening they got involved and shaped the direction, provided media coverage and provided financing through conservative right wing people like the multi billionaire Koch brothers. The net result is the Tea Party's original purpose got washed out and it became the extreme right wing vehicle of the ultra conservative Republican Party. Now we have newly elected Tea Party members in both houses of congress with little or no experience, little knowledge of economics, law, history or how congress functions and totally driven by ideology using no knowledge or logic. The people have no idea of the consequences of the actions they propose and support and don't seem to care as long as they get what their ideology demands. Their original motivation may have had merit but the current impact is at the root of the immobilizing polarization in Congress.

The Tea Party fiasco could have had positive results if they had done just a little analysis before embarking on their crusade. To take the position that all government and associated spending is bad on the basis of ideology is ludicrous. To repeal a national healthcare law that was passed because the Senate minority leader and speaker of the house denounce it without finding out it saves money and lives over 10 years is not an intelligent action. Besides, repeal harms most of them without health insurance. If you don't like it then fix it.

We have become a nation that has lost its way in too many areas and the causes are primarily political/economic. Trying to force ideologically based change whether religiously or economically based simply confuses things more and these ideological people end up being the pawns of the professional "pols". We still have many of the admirable characteristics of previous generations but more than ever our thinking has become all about money. It is not that money is bad, in and of itself, but it has come to dominate our business and politics as never before. We need to find our way again by defining what we the citizens want, not what the politicians want us to have. Our political party leadership has clearly demonstrated they want money and power for themselves and they intend to achieve that goal on the basis of our efforts and with our money. They want to continue dictating what is "good" for us and that, by the way, is what profits them. We must learn to understand the issues, the actions and the results of what they propose and stop them by forcing them to do "our business", not theirs.

CHAPTER 11

Some Ideas on Candidates

I was fascinated by the recent national televised debates of Republican presidential candidates. The most believable participant was Congressman Ron Paul who is really a libertarian, not a Republican. And the least was the front runner at the time, Mitt Romney. Neither, in my opinion offers much as the Republican standard bearer and neither would win the general election because of ideological beliefs if he were the Republican candidate. More importantly neither has any ideas or plans to bring us out of recession and put us on the path to growth and prosperity because both personal and party ideologies prevent them from having independent ideas.

Ron Paul wants the ideological Libertarian model of a much smaller government without the present services and at a lower tax rate and would eliminate a number of cabinet level departments to down size and Romny wants to be elected and will take on whatever beliefs he feels necessary to be elected. This includes denying his most important success as Governor of Massachusetts, his mandatory "Romnycare" law. Even though Mitt Romney is probably the best qualified of the candidates he is not ideologically acceptable to the radical right: for a Republican in this era of extremism, he is a moderate politically and religiously he is a Mormon, positions not popular with the radical religious right and the Tea Party. So Mitt Romny was currently being effectively challenged by the darling of the religious right, the Tea Party, Michelle Bachmann and later Herman Cain and finally Newt Gingrich and Rick Santorum.

Ms. Bachmann has done a number of admiral things in her private life including working with children as a foster parent but is so rooted in the ideologies expressed by extreme right wing Christians and the Tea party and her commitments to them she can't seem to see the needs of the country nor does she seem to care about them. Like all radicals she is devoted to her ideologies over any opposing logic and like many religious radicals that have come before her, she claims she "has been called" to pursue her cause including being the President of the United States. I assume she means that it was god or her version of god that called her and I can't verify that conversation because I wasn't there to hear the conversation and don't have his/her contact information. In any case, I find her lack of knowledge and understanding of important political issues and current problems like the consequences of defaulting on the national debt and just basic economics the poorest of the candidates. Although she makes up with for that with her dedicated constituents by virtue her animation and personal appeal it doesn't play nearly as well with independent thinkers like me. I would hope a president would bring more than just those qualities to the office, particularly a track record of "working across the aisle" to find common ground for problem resolution. Instead what I do find when I look for collaborative effort is most particularly distressing: she has fervently and consistently expressed her commitment to force us to accept her extreme right wing religious and political convictions like reversal of Obamacare and the right of women to choose and has voiced no intention of doing anything to help solve the current economic dilemma. She typifies the absurd Christian right/Tea Party, anti Obama commitment voiced by Mitch McConnell, Rand Paul and others in the House and Senate to make President Obama a "one term president", a position taken before he had even assumed the office. She not only makes no effort to find common ground to effect solutions to our problems collaboratively, she uses all her influence to polarize her colleagues to support the stated Republican campaign of maligning the president and preventing any programs that will help us pull ourselves out of the current economic mess in which the last administration left us.

Herman Cain, who makes his living as a motivational speaker, offers inane schemes of finance and tax changes that not only do no arithmetically foot, they make no economic sense whatsoever. He has looked absurd in debate and has no elected experience. His past experience as CEO of a major pizza company hardly qualifies him for foreign policy, military and political economic decisions. Now we find he has a possible/probable??? history of sexual harassment and illicit liaisons with females.

It's hard to say much good about Newt Gingrich other than he is considered very intelligent and the most effective debater by colleagues and critics alike. His track record as a congressman, Speaker of the House and political commentator/consultant and educator complicated by an erratic personal life with multiple affairs and marriages make him a poor candidate in the mind of most independent voters but at this time he is leading the field with the conservative Republican party mainly because of his outstanding use of fallacies and prejudicial rhetoric.

Rick Santorum represents the most radical of the religious right and opposes a women's right to choose plus anything that has to do with sex—contraception, family planning and education for the young. With graduate degrees in law and business he is anti-education by the state, an opponent of college for all who want it and has the most radical belief that you must not separate church and state.

They all campaign to win the upcoming election, force the party agenda on all, and feather their own nests and those of their supporters, the super-rich—not to do the peoples' business. If they are not already extreme right wing radicals they are quite willing to change their views and become radicals in order to gain the Republican nomination. What they will do afterward is the key question so we will just have to wait and see. But by espousing the ultra-conservative Tea Party and right wing religious ideologies they give living evidence they do not care about the ordinary citizen and will use the full weight of their powerful offices to further their own agenda regardless of whether it harms the country.

Strong words you say? Political bias you say? You bet they are and for good reason. The major difference between my opinions and those of the radical right and left is that my conclusions were reached doing exactly what I have urged you do when trying to understand what things mean and what "they" are saying. However, it's even easier in the case of Ms. Bachmann. She comes right out and says these ridiculous things. So step one was to listen carefully. She said she is dedicated to revoking Obamacare. She says that it's a government takeover of healthcare even though the purchase of insurance is through existing insurance companies; she says it will cost taxpayers hundreds of billions of dollars when the CBO says it will save a like amount; and she voices no concern for the 25 million Americans dependent on this new program for health insurance who would be without it if the law is revoked. In the case of women's rights to choose, her position is religious right and she expects the rest of us to follow her religious beliefs and will force them on us through government action.

So why does she take these positions? Well, she is the top congressional fund raiser, she's running for president and wants to stay on top and continue raising more money than anyone else and buy her way into the highest office in the world, the presidency of the United States. The positions she has taken attract big money because big money doesn't like the government calling shots in healthcare because they fear pressure will be brought to bring costs down and their investments and companies may be squeezed. They like high costs of healthcare. Why the tenets of the religious right? She needs their support for the nomination. So is she doing the people's business? I think not, she didn't have time to read and dissent Obamacare which she hates! She is building her war chest and support base and has not expressed concern about the people and whether they agree or whether they live or die.

Although the rest of the candidates all vary somewhat they share the common concervative philosophy of forcing their beliefs on the general population. Whether "Big Brother" in Orwell's

1984 or ultra-conservative, right-wing or ultra liberal left I must oppose what is not good for this country.

What should we be looking for in presidential candidates? First of all I believe the ideal candidate should not be extreme in his/her viewpoints and ideology. The president represents all the people and must support ideas and programs that serve all of us and all Americans in the future. And he/she should support no radical policies; we want and need responsible fiscal and social policies that invest wisely in the future. We must still build a strong middle class and eliminate poverty; these are fundamental to our culture of providing opportunity and freedom for all. Successful social programs like Social Security and Medicare need to be improved, strengthened and secured for all and our educational system needs to be updated and managed by seasoned professional teachers on a more cost effective basis that provides reasonable compensation for teachers. The candidate also needs to be well versed in international affairs and be effective in continuing to build relationships, alliances and agreements that are in the best interests of our people, including both our workers and corporate America. He/she must be well versed in economics, business and the worldwide impact of regulation or lack thereof on our country and the world. He/she must be willing and able to work collaboratively with members of all parties and especially with the congress. The bottom line is that the president must not be a radical married to an ideology of extreme thinking, either left or right if he/she is to effectively lead.

We need to think seriously about how we can help this candidate succeed when elected. The president does not rule by edict. The president rules or administers the government with the co-equal assistance of congress. If we are to be successful as a nation in the 21st century we need to elect like minded representatives to congress, regardless of party. People who share the vision of continuing as a free, prosperous and secure nation that provides the environment for growth and development of all our people. Extreme philosophies should be heard and debated and the good ideas that come from all sources should be considered and adopted when judged to be in the best interests of the majority of the people. The best places for these debates, especially radical ideas, are within the parties, at town hall meetings and when they gain strength on the floor of congress.

Unfortunately, money gets in the way of the kind of grass roots debate we would prefer. The current impact of the wealthy corporations and super-rich on grass roots developments like the recent Tea Party movement has shaped them into radical groups. Take the Tea Party for example, the super-rich Koch brothers used the promise of financial support to seed their leadership with radicals that support the super-rich and then used their financial clout to control the media to get inexperienced, unqualified and mostly uneducated radicals elected. Until we get some reduction of that impact we are going to have to look to other solutions. The best tool we have is the vote. I know, you're saying that's a "catch 22". You're right! So what's the answer?

In the best election turnouts we see only about half of eligible voters actually exercise their rights and this gives the radicals an advantage. Our answer is the large and growing number of independent voters. We need to focus on getting our neighbors on board to first understand and then support our ideas. We need to teach them what we have learned so they in turn understand

and promote understanding the issues. We need to make them aware that the only defense we have is to elect people who have the same vision of our country as we do and we need to urge them to carry the message to their friends and neighbors.

We can also join a political party and work within to attract more active members who share our beliefs. The internet offers email, twitter, facebook and blogs and instead of reading what others say, we need to say what we believe and challenge others to learn to listen, research and analyze and as we express our ideas. We also need to continually let our elected officials know we are pleased or not with the work they are doing and that we don't support radical one party solutions to the peoples' business. In other words, once we learn to understand what's being proposed we need to get into action! Remember the Constitution may teach us that all men are created equal but it does not say that all opinions of all men are equal. We need to challenge the opinions of radicals, not graciously accept them.

CHAPTER 12

So Where Are We Now?

The ideas and solutions mentioned in Chapter 10 need to be addressed now but obviously it will take time to change the nature of congress from being influenced and even controlled by outside interests to accepting their responsibility of doing the peoples' business. It will take time to make the radicals understand their day is past. We need to deal with some very important issues now. We must have tax reform, deal with the debt ceiling, the economy and disengage from the wars and it will take the best possible thinking with the least ideological bias to do these things intelligently. The problem is that at this time we have only the current cast of characters to do these things, so how do we deal with them? Remember from our earlier discussions we talked about the impact of ideological beliefs and inferred the only solution was to replace these individuals. The only thing that gets the attention of these individuals is the vote and the prospect of losing their jobs so why not take that approach. Let's identify the ideologues on both sides and bury them with email, snail mail, blogs and twitter sending strong statements demanding what we want and promising to vote for them if they support our plans and against them if they don't. Let's even go further by promising to back our demands with political contributions supporting our position. But let's even go further and form groups to elect or defeat candidates and put it out on all the communication channels. They will hear and respond, but we need to develop an integrated position on these issues consistent with our vision of what's best for the country.

So let's take these key issues and see what we can develop as our best idea for the country:

1. The most pressing issue after job creation is the debt ceiling. Conservative ideologues want to use the threat of not approving increases to control the budget and thus have unilateral control of government. The solution is simple. Use their tactic and refuse to negotiate. If we don't raise the debt ceiling we default on government payments to its creditors. By doing so we disrupt the economy, cause jobs to be lost, cost financial hardship on Social Security and Medicare recipients and seriously weaken and harm international financial markets and bring financial harm to tens of millions, maybe hundreds of millions of people around the world and the conservatives and especially the Tea Party are to blame. Let the voters know this with a strong unified voice and drive the message home through election time.

   Obviously default is not a good choice but the conservatives have caused it. There really is nothing factual to support conservative "attack and blame" arguments to the contrary and we should let the world all know that they caused the problem. We need to take a page from the conservative playbook and get on the same page as we relentlessly take this issue through to the voting booth.

Very few Americans will support conservative Tea Party candidates when they are convinced these individuals are bad for our country. Look what "Taking our country back" meant to those Tea Partyers elected in 2010. They passed a budget that the CBO classified as worsening our economy long-term; tried to repeal Roe v Wade and when they couldn't they attempted to eliminate $100 billion of programs that support the working poor, Medicaid and women's heath care services. All because of their religious ideological convictions revolving around a woman's right to choose; an issue settled almost 40 years ago. They brought nothing new to congress: they support the wars and big military spending programs, want to leave the country with no effective access to health care and in general tear down rather than build. When they "take their country back" we will look like a third world country with two social-economic classes the Super Rich and The Have Not poor with little possibility for class mobility. If you support that then the Tea Party is your answer. It most certainly is not my answer. I want a strong United States of America leading the world economically and socially with a strong middle class, no one below the poverty line and opportunities for all who are willing to work for it.

2. The economy requires three levels off support according to word renowned Nobel Prize winning economist Paul Krugman: stimulus to small business including guaranteed loans; extension of unemployment compensation; and, investment in infrastructure.

Remember we talked about how the economy creates jobs? We said our country is demand driven and we need to create more demand to cause employers to add jobs. If employers add jobs more people will spend money, that is they will consume more and that will stimulate more investment. What Mr. Krugman is suggesting is to use all of the above methods to drive consumption, create job and stimulate new investment.

The counter argument, voiced by House Majority leader Eric Cantor is tax cuts for the rich to stimulate investment and job creation and elimination of all social programs to support the working poor and unemployed. He neglects to explain that "trickle down" supply side economics has been tried by Reagan in the 80s and Bush in the 2000s with disastrous results both times. Reagan saw the error and corrected it and Bush ignored it with disastrous results. Bill Clinton realized the positive effect of balancing the budget with selected spending cuts and increased taxes on the rich and created the most prosperous decade in history and 23 million net new jobs. Cantor has no answer to those facts because his Tea Party ideology prevents individual thought and besides he is one of the thought leaders and hasn't had an original idea in recent history.

This one's a no brainer! Paul Krugman wins by a landslide and the ideologue Cantor has egg on his face for supporting a ludicrous unsupported ideological solution with a history of failure.

3. The 2012 budget has been passed in the House as proposed by Paul Ryan. It has not, nor will it be, passed in the Senate. If it were, the president would not sign it. The conservative radicals know that and are attempting to force the senate and the president to pass the Ryan plan or they will not pass the debt ceiling relief and default on the national debt the bulk of which, by the way, was created by conservative Republican presidents Reagan, Bush 1 and Bush 2. It is hard to understand why any rational, patriotic American would want to do this to his fellow countrymen and the hundreds of millions around the world that would suffer because of their misguided ideological thinking. But ideologues are not rational. These rabid right wing conservatives and Tea Partyers will do harm to us and our children and claim it is best for us because it satisfies their ideological beliefs. This has been confirmed by Michelle Bachmann, Eric Cantor, Mitch McConnell and John Boener over and over again.

These are the three vital issues that must be decided now along with numerous other problems like Medicare, Social Security and Defense spending. We also need to address immigration reform as well as and deal with the high costs and failures of our total Health Care system; and, do it with a congress that is hopelessly divided by absurd ideologies emanating mainly from the right. We need to decide what we support and take a position and let our congressional representatives know our demands.

We need to act rationally and quickly.

Group Think

We are a strange nation in many ways but nothing is more difficult for me to understand than our national inability to trust our own independent judgment. We always want others to think for us and make our decisions, and when they do we just accept it without challenging it. The South is still fighting the Civil War because they have been told things from birth that were decided wrongly by their leaders generations ago that their forbearers accepted and passed on to them. In his book "1984", George Orwell described Group Think in which leaders created stories that were accepted and believed with non-believers punished for non-conformity. We see the same thing in our organizations today. Independent thinkers are not wanted in the Conservative South, the Tea Party, the Christian Right and the Liberal left; they want absolute conformity of their members and no deviation in philosophy regardless of the negative impact on the United States. It is impossible for a member of these groups to express conflicting views and be welcomed and supported because of Group Think. Where do I go for political support if I am pro-choice, fiscally conservative; pro-immigration; pro-national healthcare; and pro-war? I am faced with the same dilemma in which Mitt Romney finds himself. It doesn't matter that he is the best qualified he fails the Group Think Test. The result is that the extreme groups that have taken over the parties have forced independent thinkers to abandon political parties. These have become the swing voters who procrastinate taking positions on key issues and indulge themselves in the lethargy of being non-voters. If we are to defeat the ideologues we need to find a way to get these individuals involved and that means we need to develop our position on issues along rational lines. Not that slogans, sub-liminal advertising and rhetoric don't work, they do and probably always will but not with the thinking voter. We must approach him/her with a logical complete argument and that means we need to have the knowledge to present to that group. We also need to convince the independent that his vote is meaningful and he doesn't have to agree with everything a candidate postulates. He needs only to find candidates that are rational and agree in intent, Differences always exist between thinking individuals and always will but rational non-ideologues will find a way to some mutually acceptable ground. Our communication program must acknowledge and even stress the desirability of those differences that can be debated and resolved.

The bottom line is that independents offer an opportunity to form alliances. As a group they see them selves as rational thinkers and will respond to a thoughtful approach based on mutual need, We can no longer trust political parties to put the peoples' business first Their own agendas have priority and while one party or the other may offer more from time-to-time we will never get the response we want without changing a number of fundamental policies and procedures defining how we elect our public servants and how we manage our government. Those of us whose opinions tend to be rational and non-biased have to lead the way. And we need to get started now.

CHAPTER 13

What Do We Change?

My immediate reaction is to suggest we fire the Congress, Administration and the Supreme Court and start over with a Parliamentary form of government. Unfortunately, that is both impractical and, short of a revolution, impossible. We have a corrupt, do nothing government because we have allowed it, and even worse, we have encouraged it by our lackadaisical attitude toward our voting rights and support of candidates who want to dismantle the system. State and local off-year elections are conducted with as little as 20% of the voters turning out to vote and national elections draw only about 50% to 60% of the registered voters. Surely we can do better than that. Perhaps we really do not understand the power of our vote.

To illustrate its importance consider what's taking place since the Republican landslide of 2010: Republican governors in fourteen states including Wisconsin, Ohio and Texas have introduced legislation to require voters to show picture ID at the voting poles on election day. Ostensibly this is to prevent voter fraud; however, when we examine the most relevant data from the law enforcement groups responsible for detecting and punishing fraudulent voters we find voter fraud to be far less than 0.1 % with heavy penalties for those who are apprehended for fraud. So if voter fraud is not the problem, what is the real reason? It is pure party politics and right up there with gerrymandering in terms of enhancing the incumbents' position. In this case the Republicans benefit because it will keep large numbers of Democratic voting Black and Hispanics from exercising their vote and discourage large numbers of young independents leaning to the Democratic philosophy as well. Why? Because they don't have picture ID and the new proposals will accept only certain kinds of ID like drivers licenses and concealed gun permits but not student IDs. Why are the Republicans pushing this? It is well known that Republican registration has declined significantly over the past 10 years with people moving to the Democratic Party or becoming independents. Political forecasters have predicted this declining party affiliation will hurt the Republicans in the 2012 elections at all levels so the Republicans are denying voters their constitutional right to vote through a well coordinated national campaign by enacting this law, which itself is probably unconstitutional. This will change the ratio of qualified voters in support of the Republican Party candidates and prevent President Obama and other democratic candidates from winning positions at all government levels. They realize their "do nothing to help the country, stop Obama at any cost to the country" strategy and their endorsement of the radical Tea Party is going to cost them a large part of the moderate voter bloc and their answer is to use their political power while they have it to consolidate their control. Their strategy is to worry about constitutionally after they win the election.

Is your vote important? The politicians think so but say your rights guaranteed by the Constitution of the United States are conditional on picture ID. I wonder what Jefferson, Adams and Washington would have to say about such an argument? I suspect they would argue vigorously against it.

So where does that leave us? What do we do about it? Or do we care at all? If we are Republican don't we gain from such actions? Let's take the last question first.

If we allow manipulation of voters rights in this instance because it favors our current goals what is the long term impact? After all, isn't the stated purpose to protect us against voter fraud? I remember the "Patriot Act" which illegally amended the constitution as a temporary solution to fighting terrorism. It's still on the books and is used as justification to implement absurd measures to "protect the public" after ten years. I went through the airport security system at Portland Oregon International Airport recently and experienced firsthand what happens when well meaning people are forced to do to implement ridiculous laws and regulations developed and ordered by incompetent leaders. I was seeing off my terminally ill stepdaughter who was returning to her husband for her final days in Nashville, Tennessee. Her picture ID driver's license was out of date because she was medically unable to drive and had been under constant care with heavy medication for over two years. This caused a major flap and a supervisor came to investigate. To his credit he finally approved her passage to the next step where she was body searched and finally allowed to proceed to the boarding area. My wife, her mother, was also body searched because she has a total knee replacement. All of this was done in the name of security despite paperwork from local medical authorities. The Patriot Act is the authorizing law for this illegal search and is itself in direct conflict with not only several articles in the Bill of Rights but the body of the Constitution defining the right of Habaeous Corpus. The Patriot Act itself is an illegal modification of the Constitution by statute law. The Constitution clearly defines how the document can be changed or amended and statute law by elected officials is not the way proscribed by the document.

Besides, we are an older couple. My wife fits the "little old lady" profile and women fitting this description have never been associated with acts of terror. So we spend billions searching for terrorists who don't exist. Remember we were attacked by Saudi radicals not little old ladies and sick women.

I remember the "Weapons of mass destruction" argument for going to war against Iraq and my heart goes out for all the death, destruction and treasury costs our nation has suffered. President Obama announced recently that after almost eleven years, more than 5000 lives lost, 30,000 wounded and Trillions of treasure expended we are finally closing down in Iraq and bringing our troops home. Once we give into bad decisions it is almost impossible to change things.

The voters' rights restrictions argument is the weakest of all excuses and probably the most dangerous act of all if allowed to prevail; because it takes away our strongest and most precious weapon in our fight against tyranny—our vote. And the reason is to stop voter fraud of less than 0.1%? Oh, I recognize MY vote is safe NOW because I have picture ID. But what about the next time a political party wants to add some other condition for voting and I don't qualify? And that will certainly happen if we don't stop it now. This is the nose of the camel in the tent as our Arab friends describe gradual encroachment. It is one more attempt at tyranny and it must be stopped at any cost! If we don't act now we will deserve even more the corruption and deterioration of our government, and we will get it!

All of the actions that take away our individual freedom and/or restrict our ability to challenge government and those who govern must be vigorously opposed. The United States Constitution clearly defines who can vote and although the act of voting and the methodology to tally votes is clearly left to the several states, the RIGHT is defined by the United States Constitution. We must oppose any conditions that take that right away. The vote is our only method of controlling our public servants. We need to pull together on this issue regardless of political party and immediately oppose the states that are placing voting controls like photo ID in place.

Things to Change

We have addressed a number of issues that are harming this country. They fall into these categories:

- Irrational radicals that drive political parties from the perspective of their radical ideologies.
- Personal agendas inconsistent with the goals and objectives that benefit all the people.
- Favoring one class to promote another with an enormous shift of United States wealth and elimination of the middle class.
- Illegal adjustment of the constitution to eliminate constitutional rights and guarantees.

The one common thread to all of these factors is money. It supports lobbyists; influences public officials running for office and controls elections. The personal gain factor is implicit in all these areas and it drives corruption and failure of our elected representatives to do the peoples' business.

Politicians would like us to believe they know best what is or is not good for the country. They try to frighten us with forecasts of doom and gloom and want us to believe they will save us if we let them have their way. It's the professional rhetoric of the politician and the current irrational message of the Republican Party that if we will just adopt their Ryan budget of slash programs and cut taxes we will miraculously recover from the current great recession. The fact that nothing in either accepted Economic theory or history supports that approach, in fact history is contradictory to that assumption. Ronald Reagan tried that in the 80s with the so called Laffer supply side, or "trickle down" economics.

Unemployment went up and GDP down until he increased taxes and took on Russia in a military deficit spending contest that put the Soviets into bankruptcy and took down the Berlin wall. He quadrupled the national debt and in the process put people back to work and positioned the United States for the rapid growth of the 90s because money was invested by the super rich to avoid taxation and not "saved" to "trickle down". Clinton with a Republican congress balanced the budget in the 90s on the basis of a high growth economy and tax increases and created 23 million jobs and countless millionaires leaving a reduced national debt of 5.5 trillion dollars. The Bush tax cuts and wars drove that to the current 15.5 trillion and the Republican party wants to go back to that policy to repair the national and international calamity created by those same policies under Bush. What kind of logic is that?

But logic is not the same as rhetoric: logic is based on facts and observation and rhetoric on the dreams and opinions of the politicians who develop the theories to achieve their personal agendas and those of their "Patronnes" not the business of the people.

It is important to note that the biggest rhetorical bogeyman they wave at us is what to do about the national debt of 15.5 trillion dollars THEY ran up. The current logic that we can cut spending and achieve a turn-around is ludicrous and supported only by the dreams of the Tea Party and the House leaders. Jobs and improving GDP are the issues, not the national debt—that's history and belongs mainly to presidents 40, 41 and 43, Reagan, Bush 1 and Bush 2.

CHAPTER 14

The Process of Change

We have talked a lot about understanding basic economics and what our political, economic and elected leaders are saying, what they are really trying to do in a political economic sense and some of the problems we see. Emphasis has been made regarding political parties and the role they play versus the role they should play, at least the role we want them to play. Finally we talked about benchmarks we can use to determine what we would change. But the question of HOW we change things has only been partially addressed. The details can be complicated and the action we take will be determined by our individual concepts of confrontation, the implied respect for authority and how strongly we feel about each individual issue. Some of us also will feel a laissez faire-do, nothing approach, saying reliance on our elected officials is preferable to a strong campaign like protesting in the streets to make our goals and programs known and supported by our elected officials. Others may believe that working within political parties is preferable; and still others may feel that contacting elected officials with email, phone calls and letters is the most appropriate. Each method will produce results if used properly, except perhaps the do nothing method. We have recent examples of these methods and we can assess the relative merits of some of these based on measurable results. In all cases it is far better to understand your own goals and objectives and what your leadership and the opposition really are saying so you can make your decision on what and who to support.

Basic Methods of Initiating Change

Fundamental to any effort to change things is a clear understanding of the law or budget item in question, the current status and what impact the proposed change would have on the law or item in question. In the case of selection a political candidate we must clearly understand his political philosophy and his stance on issues important to us. I recently heard Mr. Darrell Issa, a congressman from California comment on the second amendment to the constitution while a guest on the Bill Maher talk show on HBO. He said the reason he supports the second amendment is because it gives us a right to protect our homes and families from intruders and those who might harm us. Sound reasons, right? Maybe, but that is not what is stated in the second amendment to the Constitution. It actually is directed at what was important at that time for national defense, a well armed militia. Our powerful military and National Guard have removed our need for a militia in 2012 so even though Mr. Issa wants to own guns his support must be found somewhere else because the second amendment states:

"Amendment II
Right to bear arms
A well regulated Militia, being necessary to the security of a free state, the right of the people to keep and bear arms shall not be infringed."

**The Constitution of the United States;
p 23 American Civil liberties Union.**

So the purpose was the need for the United States to have a well regulated Militia, not to "protect home and family". This is an example of prejudiced rhetoric where the facts are distorted and presented in a way to support an argument and to convince us to agree with the author. In this case an elected official has presented false information that is broadly accepted by those that want to possess firearms and he was not challenged with the facts of the matter. If we do not want gun ownership as stated by Mr. Issa, we need to rebut the congressman's interpretation of the second amendment and we have a number of choices like You-tube, Facebook, Blogs, email to Bill Maher; letters to congressmen and to the editor of the local newspaper to name a few. We can also work to vote Congressman Issa out of office in 2012. We have a number of channels of communication and political routes to express our disagreement and we need to learn to use them. Here is an example of a false statement by an elected official that can be rebutted simply by reading the particular constitutional section and comparing what it guarantees versus what the congressman says. Easy, isn't it?

But what about other claims like the constant repetition by Republican leaders that the current administration has increased the debt to unmanageable proportions with giveaway, runaway spending and that only a program like the Ryan budget can save us from the recession, higher unemployment and financial ruin. Overwhelming statements for those of us that are just learning about how to listen and verify information and statements made by political parties. Any rebuttal requires understanding who authorized the spending, underlying causes for the spending, how the economy works and where to find the information. Remember we talked about the federal budget process in chapter 5 and learned the fiscal year for 2009, the first year of the current administration's term of office actually began on October 1, 2008 while Bush was president. A little investigation quickly validates that over $1.8trillion that was spent or committed was unplanned and spent by Bush before Obama took office. This included all the "bail-out" costs of the banks and the automobile industry; the general stimulus package to combat the unplanned unemployment increases and the costs of the wars in Iraq and Afghanistan that the Bush administration had handled with unplanned, special appropriations. These costs of over $200 billion per year were included in the 2010 budget and criticized by Republicans as unnecessary spending.

How can you validate these statements? It's easy. The budgets, fiscal years and terms of office are clearly maintained public records and available on the internet with a simple key word search. The unemployment records by month and year are available in the federal government web sites under Bureau of Labor Statistics, and the analyses of budget submission, approvals and impact are available at the Congressional Budget Office website. With that factual support we can clearly show the huge deficits of the first two years of the current administration's responsibility were heavily due to what was inherited from the Bush administration. Using the same approach we can go back through the last seven administrations beginning with Reagan's first and track the National Debt, unemployment, deficit spending and overall economic activity and clearly see where the debt originated, who was responsible and how various spending policies have influenced those results.

Why bother you say? Well, whether you are Democrat or Republican, Independent, Libertarian or Socialist you will be using the same, most accurate, facts for your analysis. There can be many opinions and many arguments can be made but only one set of facts exist that are supported by truth. If you have a vision of what you want your country to be in terms of economic strength, quality of life, freedom, income distribution and opportunity you can develop a factually based concept of what you support or oppose. You will make decisions on the basis of what you believe is best for this country and not blindly follow the party message, the talking heads and the rich and powerful. In this way you can determine how you can involve yourself, who you will support and with whom you will form alliances. In this way you can force the changes in party leadership either from within through participation or without by fighting for your candidate of choice. You will cease being a victim and be in command of your most prized possession as an American Citizen—your vote!

Change as a Tool

Part of the basic program in training managers is to instill the desire to be catalysts for change in the large or small organizations they will head. One of the thoughts I have tried to communicate to all the students and junior managers I have worked with is the absolute necessity to seek out, understand and, if possible, accept new ideas. A commitment to change in general is vital to keep organizations healthy, growing and productive. Man spends his early life continually learning new facts, new skills and new approaches to life and then as he reaches maturity, graduates from his last school and goes out into life, he begins to use what he has learned. Many of us stop learning at that point and draw whatever benefits that prior education and knowledge bring and simply accept a life of maintaining the status quo. But not all of us stop learning at this point. Not all of us accept the status quo. I think these are the winners, the movers and shakers, the ones that build new enterprises and reshape the world and never accept the status quo; they challenge, ask questions and continue to learn until the end. One of the real benefits of education is the ability to learn. What you are reading here is only the beginning. Think about what can be accomplished if you become a thinking, engaged person and add these ideas and techniques to your tool kit. The negative, biased policies of party first, dishonest government and what's in it for me can be changed and changed relatively quickly. But you can't do it alone you need allies and partners and with them you can effect change in a very short time, like before the next election . . .

A case in point is the Tea Party and what bonding together with a single message can accomplish, even if that idea is biased and non-productive. Consider what they have accomplished in a few short months within the Republican Party and, through their control efforts in that party, what they have done to the people of this country. Whether you agree with them or not learn from their success. By banding together and using the historical significance of the Boston Tea Party as a slogan, they inferred this was a new American Revolution. Using Tea Party as their name and link to historical patriotism, they successfully sold a significant portion of the US population on their "patriotic" mission and goal of "taking back" their government without ever articulating a plan. They formed alliances with others intent on taking down the government and restructuring it to suit their purposes and then cleverly took advantage of the political stalemate in congress, blaming the Democrats and President Obama, when in fact the stalemate was caused chiefly by Republican use of the filibuster in the senate. Backed by the extreme right wing Koch brothers billions and Fox news talking heads they convinced a large enough segment of the population to elect 50 plus Tea Partiers to the House of Representatives and a couple to the senate. They blamed government for all the economic and social ills in our country and based their successful congressional campaigns on "taking back" and tearing down what 225 years of working together had given us. They offered no programs to build a better country; they advocated no improvements except to cut all spending, which is another way of saying we should have no government help for anyone. When elected they stone-walled the new Republican Speaker of the House and all efforts by the Democrats to find a way to work together with Republicans to govern intelligently. The only thing they wanted was complete elimination of approximately the 15% of government spending that provides the social programs for the less fortunate in our country and Social Security and Medicare. Their message, funded by the extreme right wing conservative billionaire Koch brothers, and supported by the "talking heads" was sold so successfully we now find ourselves in the position of being held hostage by a splinter group within the Republican Party.

This action certainly re-shaped the already conservative Republican Party and moved it even further to the right. However, it has produced a Republican Party that is unable to function in a responsible, productive way. The Tea Party movement is an outstanding example of what can happen when a relatively small group of people bond together around a common political philosophy and are funded by immensely rich, radical, right wing conservatives; even when that philosophy is harmful to the future of the United States of America they can still sell it. Why? I think because most people sympathized with the "attack and blame" the Democrats strategy and as I said in the beginning of this book, people just don't get beyond the rhetoric and propaganda and really do not understand the issues. I am certain that most of those that voted for Tea Party candidates had no idea they were voting to reverse Roe vs Wade; eliminate Medicare, Medicaid and programs to help the less fortunate and all forms of social assistance programs for the unemployed, the educational system and for total obstructionism in Congress. They voted for "My way or the Highway" extreme right wing conservatives and a complete reversal of 230 years of continued social and economic progress in our country. Think of what can be accomplished when that same dedication is based on a foundation of truth and informed analysis and the learned principles are focused on and used to build a stronger, more compassionate nation.

Albeit, the Tea Party approach was successful in effecting change in the Republican Party and temporarily in the Congress; however, the way they used the communication tools of media, talking heads and internet and the message they delivered was reprehensible. They promoted hate for the President, the sitting Congress and any opposition that they found, and while well orchestrated, nothing was supported by truth and measurable facts. The resulting aftermath has seen the development of the most polarized political environment in our country since the Civil War. Their true agenda quickly became clear and as their intent inherent in the "Taking Back Government" became known and generally understood through their actions: Outlawing abortion for any reason; passing an absurd 2011 federal budget; proposals aimed at destroying our institutions; continued re-distribution of our national wealth to the super rich with the poor and middle class Americans paying the costs. Americans have begun to react throughout the country.

Granted we don't have the rich Koch brothers wanting to fund more moderate programs but we do have a large group of people who want to have responsible honest government and will work to have it. We first need to determine what we want for this country and avoid radical proposals focusing instead on what is best for the United States in terms of creating jobs, helping individuals recover from the Wall Street meltdown; getting GDP moving. Then we need to organize our thinking, set out clear goals and go find people who share our thinking and work together. We have a plethora of communication channels and there are millions like us looking for the right people with whom to form alliances. And we need to organize with new-found leaders and develop clear objectives and plans. We need to find ways to sell our programs to everyday members of both parties and especially the independents. We need all of these people in order gain enough strength to convince congress to support our positions. It's not simply a Saturday afternoon project. It will require effort and if it is to be successful we have to teach all these voters the same information contained in this book. To do that we must understand this information ourselves and be willing to bring it to others, including believing in this approach strongly enough to convince ourselves and others to contribute time, effort and money to make the message known.

CHAPTER 15

Into Action

It is time to put the things we have been discussing into action. We made it quite clear in the introduction the purpose of this book was to provide a basic understanding of Economics and Political activity, and to describe some tools and ideas to help the average person make intelligent decisions regarding economics, political issues and candidates. You bought this book or someone you respect did and gave it to you and you have had enough interest to read this far. Let's assume that is because you sincerely want to understand your government and the national economy well enough to be sure intelligent choices are being made by our elected and appointed officials and, if they are not, just how we go about replacing these representatives. You patiently read through Chapter 7 learning to hear what "they" are saying and digested a brief summary of how the congress and the macro economy works and impacts our lives. You got a little more information regarding political parties and special interest groups and how lobbyists and the super rich control so much of our government. Last, but most important of all, you were reminded of how a small group, well financed and working with a common goal can quickly impact the national scene.

As mentioned at the beginning, most Americans do not approach the responsibility of voting rationally. Nor do they develop a well thought out plan and clear understanding of the issues at hand, the impact on the country in general and on personal situations in particular. They follow the lead of their parties, talk radio radicals and the talking heads. To those of you who are expert in the areas we have been discussing who disagree with what is suggested by this book as a way to make better decisions, I invite you to do better and develop a different "how to approach" for the common American voter. We took this approach because it is our belief we can reach the largest number of voters, Democrat, Republican and Independents with information to help them understand clearly what is taking place in our country. If true, we believe voters will demand changes in campaign financing and lobbyists' activities and demand elimination of graft and outside influence on Congress. We also believe the average person can learn to recognize political rhetoric and radical behavior when they see it and cease being manipulated by talking heads and politicians.

We are also convinced that the large audiences of the television political channels MSNBC and Fox and those of the talk radio gurus, left, right, and independent will reject their influence as they learn to analytically think for themselves. We don't need more textbooks to do this but rather simple "how to" works that teach the average person of any political persuasion to make intelligent decisions and take sound political positions on important issues. Students have plenty of textbooks and they and other college graduates already have been exposed to this material and yet we have a voting population that fails to make analytical, thoughtful choices. If, on the other hand, you think what you have read has merit, then learn and understand it and then use it. As pointed out in Chapter 12, we must develop a sense of where we want our country to go and what kind of country we want to be, and do it independently from the advice of the rich and powerful and the talking heads. The material and approaches outlined in the first 12 chapters will get you off to a good start regardless of party or no party affiliation. The real subliminal message here is not to be passive about the most important thing in life—your vote, your ability to influence your country and its direction! So the second and basically unstated purpose of the book is to help generate active participation of our population and that, at a minimum, is to intelligently use our vote.

I recently heard some frightening statistics about how Americans vote, or perhaps don't vote is more correct. The substance of this report was that only about 60% of Americans eligible to vote in federal elections in the United States actually vote. I checked this out with several published sources and one, Wikipedia, stated that during the 2008 presidential election, "there were 132,645,504 total voters out of an eligible voting age population of 212,702,354, which gives you a 62.4% participation rate." http://wiki.answers.com/Q/How many registered voters in the 2008 Presidential election#ixzz1f2CdgqjF.

I am told this was considered a high percentage because voters turn out in much greater numbers for a presidential election than for off year congressional or state or local elections where voter turnout frequently is as low as 30% or less. It's hard to believe that we Americans are so misinformed, stupid or lazy that we would decline to participate and use the only real tool in our possession to ensure our freedom and way of life—our vote. But statistics don't lie.

Many explain away this lack of participation with "it's only one vote and really doesn't matter". When I have pressed these individuals for more information it quickly becomes clear that even though they usually have strong feelings about the direction our country has taken in recent years they don't know where they want things to go in the future; and, they are disgusted with party politics and feel any action on their part, including their vote, is useless. Most also have no clearly thought out expression of what they do want our country to be and offer only negative ideas to tear down government and depose the president. They want to leave the rest to professionals, like the talking heads, lobbyists and congress, the very people who brought us to where we are today, so they don't vote. As we discussed in chapter 12 we need a clear view of what we believe is best for our country and our families. Then we need to get involved, form alliances and communicate. If our individual votes were unimportant, politicians would not spend so much time, effort and money to obtain them.

Most of us don't realize just how hard parties, particularly the Republicans, are working at Gerrymandering. This is the process of redistricting congressional districts to ensure that each Congressional district has the minimum number of Republicans to ensure election of Republican candidates. The reason we single out Republicans regarding gerrymandering is because they are the minority party in terms of registration and if all voters turned out and voted a straight party ticket the Republicans would lose most elections. The Democrats will do this as well when in power and there are numerous past examples of Democrats gerrymandering but today it is the Republicans who are using that tool. So to combat this registration difference, the Republicans try to structure as many congressional districts as possible to favor as many Republicans as possible. This is handled at the state level and results in a redistribution of congressional districts' boundaries as allocated to the state based on population. If they control the legislature, as they do now in many states and, in many cases, the Governor's seat as well, they have total control and that re-distribution favors the Republicans exclusively.

After studying voter registration and voting information the party in power in that state, the Republican party, simply acts in a manner most favorable to that party. It doesn't always work to elect more Republicans but frequently it does. Sometimes the candidate supported by the party doing the gerrymandering is beaten by a well qualified opponent and instead of a gain of a seat in congress one is lost. This happened after the census in the 1990 in California when additional districts were structured as a result of increased population. The Republican party did their homework on the new Santa Barbara/Ventura congressional district, did the re-allocation and ran the long-time Republican Congressman Bob Lagomarsino in the redistricted Santa Barbara/ Ventura District, bringing in a new loyal party member, Elton Gallegly, to run in the old strongly Republican Ventura District. Congresswoman Lois Capps husband, from whom she "inherited" the seat on his death, was well known and popular in Santa Barbara and Lagomarsino was considered an interloper to Santa Barbara and lost, a good example of an informed electorate making a good decision.

This country today is in a position to make a fundamental decision regarding who we are and what we stand for. As in previous crises, the Revolution; the Civil War; World War 2; Viet Nam; and Iraq we are driven by radicals with their agendas and bombarded with the supporting rhetoric and even lies to support their programs, wars and follies and to incorporate their ideas into our values and our everyday lives. They want to change our laws to enforce their programs. They want to continue the corrupt systems that guarantee their success and they want us, the ordinary people, to bear the risks and pay the prices for their grand plans. Each side bombards us with rhetoric and fallacies and each side demeans the other and refutes any possibility of finding solutions to our national problems caused by recession, wars and unfair rewards to the super rich; and, they use every trick and fallacious argument available to them.

I made it clear in the introduction to this book that I have no party affiliation. I am still registered as a Republican in order to vote in the primaries. I resigned all positions and membership in the Republican Party in 2001. I did not leave the Republican Party as much as it left me. It has moved so far to the right that Reagan looks like a liberal. I do not support their positions nor do I necessarily support the general Democratic plans and programs. I use the methods outlined in this book and try to understand clearly the candidates, what they support; and I look carefully at the issues, their cause, our need for them and their impact on the country, the economy and my family. I recognize that most of the graft and dishonesty in government touches both parties. I also recognize the very serious problems with campaign financing, lobbying and using influence of elected office for gain are present in both parties. My position on President Obama is simple:

1. I believe he is trying to do what he believes is best for this country.
2. He is basically honest
3. He is quite intelligent
4. He is inexperienced and learning

When I compare what he has attempted and proposed to do, with the actions and proposals of Congressmen John Ryan, Speaker of the House John Boener, House Majority Leader Eric Cantor and Senate Minority Leader Mitch McConnell, I am thankful they are not in his position. Watching and listening to the current crop of presidential hopefuls I am even more grateful. Unfortunately after President Obama and Hillary Clinton the Democratic field is also weak. It is patently obvious we cannot rely on the parties and talking heads to furnish strong candidates to deliver our programs so we must dig in and start making our positions known on issues and candidates. The time will never be riper, so read and re-read what we have been talking about and put the principles into practice. Support whatever you honestly determine is best to facilitate your perception of where we should be headed as a nation that has those characteristics you believe are important; and find and support the candidates who will fight for your programs,

Good Luck!

www.ingramcontent.com/pod-product-compliance
Lightning Source LLC
Chambersburg PA
CBHW061311280526
45784CB00002B/954